AWAKENING
THE
CRYSTALS

THE ANCIENT ART AND MODERN
MAGIC OF GEMS AND STONES

SANDRA MARIAH WRIGHT
AND LEANNE MARRAMA

A TarcherPerigee Book

tarcherperigee
an imprint of Penguin Random House LLC
penguinrandomhouse.com

Most TarcherPerigee books are available at special quantity discounts for bulk purchase for sales promotions, premiums, fund-raising, and educational needs. Special books or book excerpts also can be created to fit specific needs. For details, write: SpecialMarkets@penguinrandomhouse.com.

Trade paperback ISBN: 9780593420867
Ebook ISBN: 9780593420874

Printed in Canada
1 3 5 7 9 10 8 6 4 2

Book design by Laura K. Corless

For my mother, Joanne:
You were always my rock; now I am yours.

For my husband, Kevin, who rocks my world:
"When mountains crumble to the sea, there will still be you and me."

For our beloved pug, Abigail, who snorts, snores, and wuffles
by our sides in spirit. We love you, little girl.

For my Coven, Elphame:
You are all rock stars. Shine on!

To my Gallows Hill Witchery Crystal Coven:
You each inspire and motivate me. Thank you for your kinship.

For my band, Go Your Own Way:
You continue to bring the magic and the rock 'n' roll.
"Now here I go again, I see the crystal visions . . ."

With love, dreams, and deepest gratitude,
Sandra

Our planet sustains all life.
As Earth gives to us, it is our responsibility to return what is received.
This book is dedicated to Gaia.
Thank you for sustaining, feeding, and healing your children.

Always to Rita and Eddie Marrama,
all my work is to make you proud.
Thank you both for helping me construct my dreams.
I am blessed to have you as parents.

Love,
Leanne

CONTENTS

CONTENTS

INTRODUCTION

How many items from your childhood do you still own, and of those, how many do you still use? Most of us have kept a few treasures, but they are typically tucked into a hope chest or an attic, or displayed on a shelf. But how many of them do you interact with regularly? One of my most prized possessions was given to me by my father: my first tumbled stone, a piece of fossilized coral. It has been by my side through every decade of my life, traveling with me through every move, whether it was across town or across the country. It is a relic of an ancient time in the planet's history, and it links me to the most distant days of my own story. It's one of the only things I have that my father gave me, and it holds the most meaning, because I have never stopped using it.

I have always loved crystals and gems, and along with my connection to animals, they form the basis for some of my forays into the world of magic and Witchcraft. When I was still in high school, I had a local woodworker build me my first altar, and one of the first things I did with it was create what I now know to be called crystal grids. When my family would gather for holidays, I would allow my cousins to stand at it with their hands behind their backs so they would not be tempted to touch the glittering rainbow of rocks laid out intricately in the shape of a pentacle. Tumbled stones were not expensive, and they were readily available at several shops in downtown Salem, so my collection quickly grew, along with my aspirations and the challenges I faced on the road to achieving them. My very first spell was a charm bag holding herbs and stones, and this is the same kind of working that I recommend to this day.

Decades later, I am now managing two shops in downtown Salem, watching record numbers of adults and children choose tumbled stones to help them accomplish their goals. My own company, Gallows Hill Witchery, offers larger pieces, like palm stones, wands, spheres, towers, flames, and carvings, to beginners and seasoned rock hounds alike. We have formed our own "Crystal Coven," welcoming like-minded lovers of Earth's natural treasures to live sales online that are educational as well as fun: we discuss the metaphysical meanings of the crystals, and joke around, getting to know one another and enjoying one another's company.

During the shutdown at the start of the pandemic in 2020, Leanne and I began hosting what we called Tea Time, a daily Zoom gathering that brought people together when we all felt truly isolated. I would lead everyone in a grounding and centering exercise and then pull an Oracle card, Leanne would pull a Tarot card as an action plan, and we'd discuss them. Then I'd choose a stone and Leanne would choose an herb, and we'd explain their metaphysical attributes. We did this *every single day.* Some people would take notes, while others were just happy for the kinship and resulting sense of belonging. I joked that we had become the Mister Rogers of the Witchcraft world, but I meant that in the best possible way; I was proud of the community we built. I loved sharing my knowledge of crystals and stones with the Tea Tim ers. I hope this book will capture some of that energy and deliver it to anyone who feels drawn to the magic inherent in nature's jewelry box.

—Sandra

Even though I've been a Witch for many years, crystals and stones are a relatively new passion for me. I was never a crystal freak like many of my friends. I didn't understand the obsession. I was aware that crystals provide energy to some magical tasks, but they weren't my cup of tea, no pun intended. Gifting clients a rose quartz for love or a tiger's eye for protection thrilled them, and a large amethyst I had been given by a friend decorated my living room. But beyond that, crystals were pretty rocks that adorned my altar or psychic reading table. I never really worked with them.

When Sandra and I started writing our first book, *Reading the Leaves*, we would occasionally suffer writer's block, and Sandra was quick to turn to her stones for help. Her extensive knowledge of gems and crystals intimidated me. Her hands and neck are always adorned with sparkling jewels, and any time we hit a wall, she sat with her stones, got inspired, and called me with her breakthrough idea. That enthusiasm was contagious, and soon we'd be off and running again. It became clear to me then: crystals were calling me. First, I put my citrine ring on my finger to warm up to the writing process and stimulate my creative mind. Next to my computer, I placed fluorite so I could focus on my own individual story, and an aventurine stone to open my mind to inspiration. Armed with my newly charged thoughts and ideas, powered by the gifts from the earth, the book took shape.

In 2020, like for so many of us, my life turned upside down. Everything I held on to started to fall apart. I turned to the earth to give me the grounding, strength, and healing I needed. In June, my daughter had a grand mal seizure. She was completely unresponsive as I watched her tremble uncontrollably on the floor. I helplessly watched the ambulance take her away; due to COVID-19 restrictions, I was unable to follow her to the hospital.

Forced to sit and wait for any news of her status or diagnosis, I turned to crystals to channel my energy, both to help my child heal and for me to stay sane while I waited for any news of her condition. Using my instinct, I held on to an amethyst tower, letting the calming energy keep me from jumping into the car, driving to the hospital, and breaking down the door to get to her (I honestly considered it more than once). As I clutched the amethyst, I visualized my daughter. I sent her nervous system peace and stability. I'd like to say I had some deep and meaningful mantra, but I just rocked back and forth for what felt like hours, repeating, "Be okay, please be okay," until I got the call that she was, in fact, going to be okay and she could return home. The day after she returned, I got her a black jasper necklace to help heal her nervous system.

It was only a month later that my boyfriend was rushed to the hospital with non-COVID-related lung issues. He was in the ICU for over a week. I thought I was going to lose my mind. That is when Sandra gifted me a bloodstone, a mineral used frequently for physical and emotional healing. These days, my boyfriend is on the mend, and that bloodstone stays under our mattress so he can receive its blessings (and I can stay sane).

Around the same time, crystals and stones also helped me gather my strength to leave a successful position as a psychic and to start building my own business. Crystals were either in my pocket, around my neck, or in my bra as Pentagram Shoppe was created. Hematite helped me keep my ADD in check. Rose quartz helped me communicate with my friend and business partner, Tim. Citrine and aventurine kept the creativity and money flowing so we could open successfully on October 1, 2020.

Once crystals and stones became more than just decorations in my life, I discovered something pretty amazing: Crystals *want* us to use them. They have become my batteries and the fuel that aids me in my work as a psychic, especially as a medium. As a lover, I have used crystals to put the extra special zap in the bedroom. As a mother, I have used stones to provide protection and calming to my children. As a friend, I have used them to heal and give peace to people I love. I have discovered that crystals arrive in our lives when we need them. The more I work with them, the more I grow with the spirit of our planet. Now I want to share that gift with you.

—Leanne

1

OLD AS DIRT: THE RELATIONSHIP BETWEEN PEOPLE AND STONES

One of the literal building blocks of our planet, stone was here long before we were. Layers and layers of it form the basis of our world, and the markedly beautiful specimens have been among our most prized possessions since their discovery thousands of years ago. Crystals and gemstones show up in our holy books, and they have adorned the crowns of rulers of the most formidable empires ever to rise and fall. Crystals have powered everything from ancient Sumerian magical formulas and traditional Chinese medicine three thousand years before the Common Era to the computers we typed these words on. Ancient Egyptians buried pharaohs with vibrant lapis lazuli, carnelian, emerald, and turquoise adornments and ritual tools; Asian emperors went to their graves wearing jade armor. Gems have always accompanied the eminently powerful among us as they embarked on the most mysterious journey of all, bestowing protection and blessings into the Great Beyond.

For centuries, gemstones have functioned as the physical representations of our intentions, visual reminders of our desires, and the touchstones of our dreams—those we have made manifest and those we have yet to attain. Across Earth's continents, they are prized for their beauty, perceived value, and the stories they tell, as they are handed down through the generations. Many famous amulets contain gems, and often the gems themselves are considered to be talismans of wondrous or fearsome power.

A Girl's Best Friend

Sandra: *At the beginning of every Amulets and Talismans class I taught in Salem, I always asked the attendees, "Is anyone wearing a talisman right now?" If there were a couple of Witches present, their hands would shoot up and everyone else would look around the room to see who these magical creatures were. I would then say, "How many of you are wearing a wedding ring?" A talisman can be a symbol of a commitment to be understood by all who see it, a protection of sorts against unwanted attention, a daily reminder of a promise made and kept, and more. It is a bit of magic, truly, and the stones chosen for engagement rings and wedding bands are typically those that have long been associated with devotion, fidelity, honor, passion, and, of course, love. The most common choice these days, diamonds, are among the hardest substances on the planet, and their strength, longevity, and luster embody what we all hope for in our relationships.*

There are a few select gemstones that have captured the imaginations of generations, and one in particular is the queen of them all: the Hope Diamond. The blue jewel is just over 45 carats, valued at about a quarter of a billion dollars—and said to carry a curse for anyone who would claim ownership or dare to touch it. Its origin story goes like this: Stolen from the brow of an idol by a corrupt priest in a temple in India, it passed through the hands of nobility and notoriety, eventually landing in the inheritance of its namesake, British politician Henry Thomas Hope. The dazzling gem left a bloody trail in its wake, which included the beheadings of Marie Antoinette and Louis XVI. Many of the misfortunes attributed to the stone have never been verified, but the tales of divorce, disease, destruction, and death remain a warning against the pitfalls of theft, greed, and sacrilege, and this lore showcases the power that people have placed in gemstones through the centuries.

YOUR OLDEST STONE COMPANION

It's a pretty safe bet to say that you know your birthstone. You were probably given something featuring your birthstone when you were growing up; it is often one of the first pieces of jewelry we receive. You may have even been told that wearing it would bring you good luck. Did you ever stop to think about why that stone was associated with your birth month or your zodiac sign?

We each own a copy of the updated version of *Love Is in the Earth* by Melody, which was printed in 1995. This book runs between $50 and $200 used, but Sandra got hers back when it was still in print; it came highly recommended, and she immediately understood why. It is in the all-time top five comprehensive books on crystals when it comes to their metaphysical properties. One of the themes that emerged right away was that several of the stones we love and wear in our jewelry are purported to have adorned "the breastplate of the high priest." (This has almost become a running joke over the years, as Sandra has remarked more than once that she would love to see this breastplate because it would probably be absolutely stunning.)

The high priest in question was Aaron, the first high priest of the Hebrews, and his breastplate contained twelve gems, one for each of the twelve tribes of Israel. The stones were said to be set in four rows, each containing three stones. This is particularly interesting because there are four groups in the zodiac: signs of air, fire, water, and earth, and they are organized into three types: cardinal, fixed, and mutable. The first writings we know of that associate the gems in the breastplate with the signs of the zodiac come from Flavius Josephus in the first century of the Common Era. As you might imagine, the list of stones is not exactly definitive, and even Josephus changes the lineup in his writings; but one description of the grid details that "the first three stones were a sardonyx, a topaz, and an emerald. The second row contained a carbuncle [garnet], a jasper, and a sapphire. The first of the third row was a ligure [zircon], then an amethyst, and the third an agate . . . The fourth row was a crysolite [peridot], the next was an onyx, and then a beryl."

The modern list of birthstones has changed, too. It was first codified by the National Association of Jewellers in 1912, and it has been updated in the last decade in both the US and the UK. The stones that we were taught when we were growing up were garnet for January, amethyst for February, aquamarine for March, diamond for April, emerald for May, pearl for June, ruby for July, peridot for August, sapphire for September, opal for October, topaz for November, and turquoise for

December. There are several "alternate" stones, too, including pink tourmaline for October, more than likely because opals have a reputation for being unlucky (specifically, they were thought to bear a curse that could bring about death, although some say that the curse doesn't apply to those born in October, or doesn't apply if the stone was given as a gift). Much like the tales surrounding the Hope Diamond, compelling stories—fictional and otherwise—have contributed to the layers of lore around this multicolored stone.

The association of luck with certain gems worn at specific times has likewise developed and changed, with some cultures believing it is good luck to wear the stone associated with a zodiac sign during the period when the Sun is in it. Stones may be worn to support health or to help face life's challenges. This is a part of our practice today, and it forms the basis for this book. From marking milestones to gravestones, rocks are both useful tools and luxurious jewels, bringing beauty and bestowing blessings. Crystals can protect, heal, empower, and transform those who understand how to awaken their potential and, in turn, the magic within themselves.

2

CHOOSING, CONNECTING, CHARGING, AND CLEANSING

We have counseled hundreds of clients on finding the right stone for whatever they were working on, whether that's something they hoped to change, bring into their lives, or get rid of. Many factors go into the decision to work with a particular crystal, and choosing can be a daunting task: There are thousands of stones that come in every shape and size, and, frankly, the available information about their metaphysical properties can be a boring read. There are a lot of comprehensive resources out there, but many of them are not much more than a long alphabetical list of crystals, photos that show you how to identify them, and a string of keywords to explain what they are known for.

Truth be told, we have never once picked out a crystal based on that kind of advice. In fact, more often than not, it's the crystal that chooses us. We gravitate toward a stone and only later discover that it was exactly what we needed at the time.

Sandra: *Long before I ever purchased a book on crystals, I would walk into shops where they were sold and learn about their properties by the signs tucked into the display containers—but I also sensed things about them. I found I was instinctively "reading" the stones, many times before I even held them or saw the information on the placard. Understanding the significance of different colors gave me an advantage, but I also picked up on characteristics that I could not have known without psychic communication. The first time I held a lepidolite, I called it "the giggle stone" because it lifted my spirits and made laughter bubble up inside me. I later learned that it contains lithium, which has long been used as a mood stabilizer and a treatment for depression, among other things.*

When it comes to choosing stones, our first piece of advice is this: Trust your gut. If you are drawn to a crystal, it has something to teach or offer you. Do some research, and decide why it has come to you at this moment. It may be a stone that you need for only a short time, or it may become a lifelong companion; but there's a reason it sought you out, and finding out why can give you key information about your present situation.

If there's a particular issue that you're working on and you want to find crystals that can help you achieve a specific goal, there are a few steps we recommend you take to ensure a successful match.

Awaken a Companion Crystal for Spellwork

1. Define your goal as specifically as you can. Write it down on paper or in your journal.

2. Determine the type of help you want, which may mean choosing a combination of crystals.

3. Choose the crystal(s) based on your intention(s). Refer to the glossary on page 187 for a comprehensive list.

4. Decide on the most useful size and shape. Are you carrying the stones with you, or placing them in a particular area?

5. Cleanse the crystal to remove any residual energies it has picked up in its travels. Learn how on page 20.

6. Charge the stone to imbue it with your energy, and outline how you want it to assist you. See page 20 for instructions.

7. Carry it, place it into a crystal grid, or set it in your space to absorb its energy.

Let's go through the types and shapes of stones that will allow you to make the most of their energies in any situation. In the following chapters, we will suggest crystals for the goals and challenges we have encountered most frequently in our own practice and explain how to put them to work in all areas of your life. We have also included an at-a-glance guide at the end of the book that you can reference whenever you are ready to enlist the help of these amazing stones.

Come as You Are—Crystals, Unplugged

Some crystals don't need any #filter: They are sold pretty much the way they appear in the mine.

Rough or "raw"—these crystals have not been processed or altered in any way. Think of them as the fresh vegetables of the crystal world: They are as they grew in the earth. Their unadulterated nature gives them a pure feel. Some are small enough to carry in your pocket. Others are larger, like . . .

Clusters—naturally formed groupings of crystals, with many points capable of sending energy from the base into multiple directions simultaneously. They are also a fabulous choice for keeping the vibrations of a room high.

Geodes—a hollow rock, typically cut in half to reveal an interior lined with crystal formations and a "rind" of agate.

FOR WHEN YOU WANT TO PUT A LITTLE EFFORT IN: A POLISHED LOOK

Tumbled—these are the smooth, shiny stones you see in bowls or bins in metaphysical shops. They retain the same properties as their raw counterparts, but they have been polished to enhance their appearance and make them smooth to the touch, which makes them easier to work with if they are to be placed on the body (no sharp edges!). If a crystal has a hardness of 5 or above, it can be tumbled in a rotary or vibratory tumbler over a multistep process that takes about one full moon cycle, which we think makes these stones even more magical. Due to their size, they are better suited for personal use rather than to cover an entire area with energy. If you want the energy to spread out over a room-size area, you'd be better off choosing . . .

Freeform/altar stones—these large, polished pieces are like giant tumbled stones (they remind us a little of Stonehenge). One edge is typically flat so they can stand up. Their stature makes them a good choice for creating an aura in a room. You can also hold smaller versions, but if you're looking to regularly work with a decent-size stone in your hands, you should get a selection of . . .

Palm stones—named after exactly what they are designed for, these stones are the best to hold during meditation. Try resting one in the cup of your palm or gripping it in your closed fist to make sure it feels natural and comfortable in your hand. If you want something a bit more portable that you can rub to reduce stress and promote a sense of calm, you may want to consider . . .

Worry stones—the fidget toys of the mineral kingdom, these typically oval stones have a thumb-size groove that you can rub to discharge excess energy and relieve anxiety. They are small enough to discreetly fit into a pocket, so they travel well. Worry stones are arguably one of the most perennial ways humans have used crystals, as the practice dates back as far as ancient Greece, when the stones would be smoothed by running water, and further by frequent use.

This brings us to the many ways that stones can be carved to give them another layer of meaning and purpose.

Decorative stone carving has been around since prehistoric times. Crystals have been sculpted into everything from idols of worship to representations of geometric shapes, animals, and even utilitarian forms like sinks and bathtubs. The following shapes are the ones we have personally used or recommended to our clients:

Cubes—the most stable of shapes, cubes are champions at grounding and/or holding energy. Their "building block" ap- pearance is a visual cue to remember to lay a firm foundation in your goal setting. Cubes invite in security, strength, support, consistency, and determination.

Pyramids—combine the strong foundation of the square with the manifestation energy of the triangle and you've got the power of the pyramid. The topmost point directs energy upward, raising the vibe in any room, and the shape reminds us that we are the rulers of our own destiny. When you are ready to take charge of a situation, this is the shape to reach for.

Spheres—round silhouettes call to mind the shape of planets, a feeling of wholeness, the idea of unity, and the circle of life, death, and rebirth. A sphere is also the shape of a traditional crystal ball, which earned its own emoji as an icon of psychic ability due to its association with scrying (think crystal ball gazing). Hold smaller spheres in your hands when you are actively sending energy, or set them in a stand, where they can passively emit vibrations in all directions. A sphere's bubble of influence will grow when you work with it. The more energy you invest, the greater the area its energy will cover. *Sandra: These are one of the most popular shapes at Gallows Hill Witchery. Some of the members of the Crystal Coven have entire sphere gardens, which inspired me to create my own in my living room.*

Mirrors—exactly what they sound like. Whether flat or curved, mirrors are made out of reflective stones like obsidian for the practice of scrying, which we will delve into in chapter 9. These are almost always round, but you may find them carved into celestial shapes.

Pendulums—these cones are suspended from a chain, ribbon, or strand and are used to visualize psychic energy into information. (We will go into greater detail about how to use them in chapter 9.) Pendulums are smaller versions of . . .

Points—these sharp crystals can be used to channel energy in a single direction: out the pointy end. They are the arrows of the crystal world, and they help focus your aim, much like . . .

Wands—points that are specifically designed to be held in the hand to direct energy are called wands, and they have been used for centuries as a tool to manipulate and direct energy.

The concept of the magic wand has been around since ancient times, when certain gods were depicted holding rods or scepters as a symbol of power and dominion. Crystal wands help you channel your energy to create sacred space, to cleanse or bless objects (including other crystals), and in psychic healing. Astrologically speaking, we appreciate "big wand energy" and suggest that any fellow cardinal signs try working with wands—we're looking at you, Libra (air), Aries (fire), Cancer (water), and Capricorn (earth). A wand also makes a great massage tool, much like . . .

Eggs—not just for breakfast! Egg-shaped stones symbolize the divine feminine, so you may place them on your altar to represent the Goddess, and remind yourself of your sacred connection to Her. The slimmer end can be used in reflexology or acupuncture, particularly to detect and rebalance energy blockages in the body.

Towers—these are perfect sentinels, standing guard and continuously raising the vibration in any area. They bring a sense of security—particularly when made from a grounding or protective stone—and stability, so they also work well when created from stones that influence relationship, financial, health, or other concerns. Heads up to our friends who are the fixed signs of the zodiac—Aquarius (air), Leo (fire), Scorpio (water), and Taurus (earth)—this shape is totally your vibe: capable, steadfast, powerful, and reliable.

Flames—similar in stature to the tower but with a fiery shape that suggests mobility and movement and can introduce the attributes of fire to your crystal grid or spell. Combine a crystal flame with a spell candle to give any working extra oomph. It's also the crystal to reach for if you need to get out of a rut, because it is all about action, change, and transformation—much like the mutable signs of the zodiac: Gemini (air), Sagittarius (fire), Pisces (water), and Virgo (earth).

Hearts—crystals formed into the universal symbol of love are often given as gifts, carried to attract or strengthen relationships, or used in workings relating to healing, particularly cardiac health. They can signify specific people in a crystal grid: family or coven members, lovers, spouses, or friends.

Carvings—this umbrella term covers the menagerie of animals, angels, and other entities that are carved from hundreds of different kinds of crystals and stones. They vary in size from 1 or 2 inches to a foot tall, or even larger, and they are used to connect with the traits of the creature depicted. They can be carried or placed on an altar or in a crystal grid to invoke the spirit's power and ask for its assistance.

Skulls—quite possibly the most controversial shape of all, these may depict human, animal, or extraterrestrial craniums. Certain crystal skulls have even become famous through the telling and retelling of their stories, but none are from the lost city of Atlantis or other planets or stars, nor from documented excavations. Many were carved in Germany from crystal mined in Brazil, so while the stones might be ancient, the carvings are from the 1800s or later. Their stories, no matter how outlandish, have common themes that can teach us things that will help us become better as individuals, communities, and societies. They remind us of our mortality, encourage us to honor our ancestors, support our efforts to heal ourselves and others, highlight the value of knowledge, and can facilitate communication with those we love who no longer have physical form on this plane. (Sandra is what is known as a skullkeeper: She has what she calls a Council of Skulls housed on her ancestral altar in her temple.) We will talk more about how to build a relationship with a crystal skull in chapter 9.

REGULARLY SCHEDULED MAINTENANCE: CLEANSING YOUR CRYSTALS

Like all physical objects, crystals and stones attract dust, so they periodically require physical cleaning. But they are also metaphysical objects that pick up energy, which need to be cleansed as well (with a few exceptions, which we will talk about later in this chapter—see Crystal Cleansers on page 22).

Carefully clean your crystals with a dry, soft cloth; microfiber will gently remove dust without damage. Choose a color you don't use for other things and designate that as your crystal cloth to avoid cross-contaminating with cleaning products, which are not necessary and may be too harsh for your stones.

WHAT IS CLEANSING AND CHARGING A CRYSTAL?

You don't have to consider yourself a Witch to cleanse and charge a crystal, or any other object. You just have to understand how energy works, and why we do it.

To cleanse a crystal is to clear it of any residual energy it may have picked up in its travels. Prior to working with it, you can pass it through the smoke of frankincense and myrrh, sage, or palo santo, depending on what is a part of your spiritual practice. (We recommend frankincense and myrrh to our clients who are just starting out, and we use it ourselves.)

To charge a crystal is to imbue it with your own energy in accordance with its properties. Some people place crystals in moonlight or lay them on an object meant for charging; this is a *passive* way to charge a stone, because it is absorbing energy from light or from an object that is not deliberately, consciously directing it. It is a general blessing.

To charge the crystal for a *specific* purpose, use an *active* method, such as holding it between your palms and focusing your intent on it. If you can focus and feel your energy, you can charge a crystal. If you have never felt your own energy, this is one way to explore it: Clap your hands and rub them together for ten seconds. Hold your palms about an inch apart, then move them to about 5 inches apart, then back to about an inch apart, and note how you can feel your hands getting closer and moving away. If you have a hard time feeling it with your eyes open, close them, which should make it easier. This will help you practice channeling your energetic power through your hands.

To charge a crystal both actively and passively at the same time, you can lay it on a charging plate and place your dominant hand (the hand you write with) over it, sending the energy through your palm. You can use these methods to prepare your crystals before doing any of the spells in this book.

THE FIVE SACRED ELEMENTS FOR CLEANSING CRYSTALS

Air: bathing crystals in the smoke of incense associated with purification and blessing, like frankincense and myrrh

Fire: passing crystals over the flame of a candle that has been blessed for that purpose

Water: immersing crystals in clean water, often blessed by sunlight, moonlight, or other methods. Check to make sure the crystal you're cleansing is water-safe. See the list of water-safe crystals on page 91.

Earth: placing crystals in salt or on a charging plate, which is usually made of a cleansing stone, such as selenite

Spirit: along with any of the other elements, using your own personal energy to purify the crystals

CRYSTAL CLEANSERS

There are two crystals that we recommend to purify other crystals for energy work: selenite and kyanite.

Selenite—a form of gypsum, selenite was named by the ancient Greeks after the Moon Goddess Selene. It never needs to be cleansed, as it does not hold on to any undesirable energies it comes into contact with, and it is easy to form into a variety of flat shapes that can be used for cleansing, known as **charging plates.** It's a good thing that selenite doesn't require cleansing, as it is water-soluble, so don't get it wet for any length of time or it will begin to dissolve.

Kyanite—this crystal is a silicate, and like selenite, its salty nature makes it ideal for purification and it never requires cleansing. Its name also has Greek roots: *kuanos*, meaning "blue." If you do energy work, Reiki, or follow any system that includes the chakras (energy channels in the body), a kyanite wand will help remove blockages and restore balance. It can also be used to actively cleanse objects or stones, and can passively keep your crystals ready for whenever you need them.

AN IMPORTANT FINAL NOTE ABOUT CLEANING METHODS

When choosing crystals for metaphysical purposes, be sure to pay attention to their physical characteristics, too. Softer stones may dissolve or break up in water, and some, like malachite, can even make water toxic. Crystals with high metal content (e.g., pyrite, hematite, magnetite) and any stone that feels porous or soft to the touch, like opal, fire opal, amber, lapis, azurite, turquoise, or apatite, should not be submerged. Stones with a flaky or crumbly texture, like kyanite, raw black tourmaline, gypsum, desert rose, calcite, celestite, lepidolite, or apophyllite, do not belong in contact with water at all. (There are sinks made of labradorite, but they have been specifically treated for it.) Likewise, moonstone, kunzite, and amazonite may be damaged by water. **When it comes to water and crystals, knowledge is power; when in doubt, leave it out.**

3

#GOALS:
YOUR CRYSTAL COMPANIONS

The stones that are most energetically active are the stones that go everywhere with you. Tucked into a pocket, purse, or bra, these are the allies that help you tackle each day. Many people have their "ride or die" crystals with them all the time, for everything from protection to attraction, to boost personal power or to bring peace and comfort. Crystals remind us of our intentions, helping us stick to the path that will lead us to our goals. Think of them as teachers, reminding us to look inward, and keeping us on track mentally and psychically as we manifest our hopes and dreams.

Your Daily Crystal Complements, Colleagues, and Cohorts

The closer a person is to the energy field of a crystal, the more effective that crystal becomes. The most powerful way to receive energy from an object is by touching it, and skin-to-crystal contact provides a direct connection to a stone.

To make the most of these benefits, crystals can be worn as jewelry or carried in other creative ways. Leanne always has several crystals in her bra for strength, healing, protection, and luck. For people who don't wear bras, try your jacket, shirt, skirt, dress, or pants pockets, which still keeps your stones close at hand and builds a bond with them. You may even place one in your wallet or handbag, which is especially effective for abundance, protection, or success work, and controlling unnecessary spending. Leanne has a client who tapes crystals to her smartphone to curb online shopping and stem the tide of boxes that arrive at her house.

You Wear It Well: Crystal Bling

Jewelry is magic you can take with you wherever you need to attract, maintain, or deflect energy, and different styles (rings, bracelets, earrings, necklaces) work a bit differently. Wearing crystals keeps them in constant contact and visible throughout the day. The unique brilliance of each stone brings confidence to the wearer, and its beauty amplifies and extends our natural gifts.

While choosing what crystals to wear, consider the flow of energy that comes from the different areas of the body. Wearing specific stones on certain areas can help shift and control that current. Each side of the body holds a distinct power, and each part of the body is associated with particular abilities as well.

Crystal rings or bracelets worn on your dominant hand (the one you most often write with, commonly the right hand) will manifest changes, create transformation, wield protection, and generate influence. This hand has predominantly masculine energy and is known as the **projective** hand. Crystals worn on the dominant side of your body will assert your influence over a situation and bring your desires to fruition.

Stones and crystals on the nondominant side of your body receive energy. Choose these crystals carefully, as they influence the energy you absorb from external sources. Wear stones here to welcome in healing, good luck, wealth, love, happiness, and more. Your non-dominant hand has predominantly feminine energy and is known as the **receptive** hand. If you tend to worry, stones worn on this side will reduce emotional stress, ease anxiety, and promote inner peace.

The same crystals can be effective for different reasons when worn on each side of the body. Rose quartz worn on the nondominant side can help you love yourself more, but if you're looking to receive love, it should be worn on the dominant side to project that desire outward. For those of us who live with attention deficit disorder, fluorite is especially helpful when worn on the receptive side, neutralizing harmful emotions, such as stress and self-doubt, and boosting confidence and concentration. Carry it when learning new information, to hone your focus and listening. When worn on the projective side, fluorite will help you deliver your thoughts and ideas effectively to others. As always, working with both sides of the body—of anything, really—is the key to balance.

RAISE YOUR HANDS: CRYSTAL RING MAGIC

A ring is a symbol of supremacy and power. The circular shape represents unbroken unity and completion, perpetuity and commitment. This can be a devotion to the self, another, or a deity. Each finger is associated with a magical purpose, so you can wear rings on different fingers to give power to whatever you are trying to manifest.

INDEX FINGER

The index finger is also known as your pointer, directing you toward opportunities and adventures. It is ruled by **Jupiter,** the planet of expansion and good fortune. Wear rings on the receptive index to invite in fresh avenues for income and worthy business partners, and on the projective index to manifest success and influence powerful leaders. Whether you're going to a job interview, playing games of chance, or investing, consider wearing blue lace agate, lapis lazuli, sapphire, or turquoise.

MIDDLE FINGER

When someone gives someone else the finger, it's a clear display of authority. The middle finger embodies your personal power. (It certainly makes a statement when directed at other drivers on the road, although we do not endorse this.) It is governed by **Saturn,** a planet referred to as "The Great Teacher of the Zodiac," so rings worn on the receptive side instill responsibility, discipline, and self-control, and on the projective side exude command, expertise, and sovereignty. If you're a teacher, a CEO, or in law enforcement, take control over any situation with black onyx, obsidian, or shungite on the middle finger.

RING FINGER

The ring finger is connected to the life-giving, illuminating light of the **Sun,** which brings loving warmth and growth to all. The ancient Romans believed that the ring finger contained a vein directly connected to the heart and could influence affection. We still express love and commitment by wearing engagement and wedding bands here to symbolize the promise of eternal love. Wear rings on the receptive ring finger to connect with your passions, welcome in healing energy, and receive divine guidance, and on the projective side to shine with self-confidence, particularly when performing for an audience or showcasing your talents in the arts.

Some brilliant crystals for the ring finger are amber, citrine, diamond, ruby, sunstone, and tiger's eye.

PINKY FINGER

The smallest digit communicates a big statement to the Universe. Ruled by the planet **Mercury,** the little finger is related to social life and the attitude that you carry toward the rest of the world. It supports inspiration and mental processing, and it helps writers and public speakers articulate their thoughts and ideas. Wear rings on the receptive side to aid with mental clarity, memory, and perception, and on the projective side to communicate clearly and effectively.

Try alexandrite (the way the stone changes color in different forms of light is perfect for Mercury), carnelian, orange calcite, kyanite (especially orange), or labradorite (especially bicolor or multicolored flash).

Note: The pinky is the finger that has the most contact with outside surfaces, with nothing on its edge to guard it (unlike the index finger, which enjoys the protection of the positioning of the nearby thumb). Be extra careful when wearing expensive or sentimental pieces on this finger.

THE THUMB

The thumb is unique in that it contains the powers of both **Venus** and **Mars**, the planetary symbols of the feminine and masculine energies, respectively.

The thumb is associated with logic and will, and the ego. It is the part of the hand that emanates a person's self-identity, and a symbol of human development and scientific progress. (We're thinking of that old joke: If cats had opposable thumbs, they'd have already taken over the world.)

If you want to lean into your masculine side, crush your competition, overcome inertia, rev up your sex drive, or engineer a breakthrough, wear a ring on your dominant thumb and leave your nondominant one unadorned. If you want to draw on your feminine powers, attract love and abundance, express your artistic creativity, give birth to new ideas and projects and nurture them to success, do the opposite. For balance, wear a ring on each side, like Sandra does; she rarely ever takes off her thumb rings.

For a big thumbs-up, go for Venus/feminine stones like aventurine, chrysocolla, emerald, kunzite, peridot, or rose quartz, or Mars/masculine stones like bloodstone, fire opal, garnet, or hematite.

BRACE YOURSELVES:
CRYSTAL WRIST BLING

Throughout history, people have worn bracelets and armbands for many reasons: to announce allegiances, symbolize unbroken love and friendship, or for practical protection as part of armor. Growing up, we exchanged friendship bracelets woven from embroidery floss and decorated with beads. These days, we stack our wrists with gemstone bracelets: They are one of the most popular items in our live sales, and with good reason. Bracelets are an easy—and fashionable—way to stay connected to the crystals you are working with, keeping them against your pulse points and in your line of sight.

The gems you wear on your receptive, nondominant wrist bring their magic to you, and those you wear on your projective, dominant wrist manifest your desires. As you plan what to wear, decide which stones will bring you the energy you need to fuel your day, and which ones will help you master it.

One way to amplify your magic (or even link it with someone else's) is to wear a bracelet made of the gemstones associated with specific signs of the zodiac. If you are into astrology, try pairing your sun sign and your partner's, or have your birth chart done and wear a trio of your sun, moon, and rising signs.

CRYSTALS OF THE ZODIAC

The dates for each sign are approximate because they vary slightly each year due to the slight changes caused by Earth's orbit. Also, a special note to those born on the cusp of two signs: have a professional astrologer do your chart with your exact time and place of birth to see which sign your Sun truly falls in.

Aries (the Ram): March 21–April 19: These fiery leaders glow in carnelian and red jasper.

Taurus (the Bull): April 20–May 20: These stable, dependable stalwarts shine in aventurine or emeralds.

Gemini (the Twins): May 21–June 20: The dual nature of these air signs dazzles in alexandrite, and chrysocolla harmonizes their two sides beautifully.

Cancer (the Crab): June 21–July 22: This sign is all about the Moon, so moonstone fits these sensitive homebodies best, but you also can't go wrong with pearls.

Leo (the Lion): July 23–August 22: These lionhearted solar cats beam with tiger's eye and pyrite.

Virgo (the Virgin): August 23–September 22: Mercury's laser-focused taskmasters love fluorite as well as the traditional sapphire, especially for September babies.

Libra (the Scales): September 23–October 23: Venus's favorite charismatic mediators should try pink tourmaline or opal.

Scorpio (the Scorpion): October 24–November 21: These intense and intuitive enigmas vibe with flashy labradorite and smoky quartz.

Sagittarius (the Archer): November 22–December 21: Fiery citrine ignites these free spirits, and turquoise will protect and balance any ambitious adventurer.

Capricorn (the Goat): December 22–January 19: These resilient entrepreneurs operate best with garnet and jet.

Aquarius (the Water Bearer): January 20–February 18: Air's deep-thinking peacekeepers speak through high-vibration amethyst and angelic celestite.

Pisces (the Fish): February 19–March 20: Tranquil aquamarine and soothing blue lace agate suit these creative changelings.

SPEAK YOUR MIND AND CROSS YOUR HEART: CRYSTAL NECKLACES AND PENDANTS

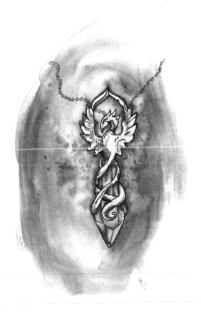

Crystal necklaces and pendants have functioned as talismans and amulets since ancient times. The first necklaces were made of natural substances, such as shells, stones, and seeds, and often served ritualistic purposes as well as revealing a person's position and rank in society. Even today, necklaces are often status symbols, indicating influence and affluence. Once you get to know the metaphysical properties of various stones and crystals, you can communicate your own ideas and messages through this highly visible location—or keep some things to yourself by wearing them under your clothes.

Crystals kept close to the throat stimulate communication and dialogue, so hang them around your neck to hear their messages and boost your own. They can illuminate what is being said, increasing the power of spoken words. (Sandra has a bronze torc with a labradorite stone on each end, which sit on either side of her voice box, just below her ears. When wearing it, she can speak with spirit and hear the voices on the other side.) Worn over the heart, crystals amplify the unspoken language of love and guard against emotional harm.

To work on overcoming shyness, social anxiety, and other obstacles to self-expression, wear these pendants near the throat:

Air signs (Gemini, Libra, Aquarius): angelite, apatite
Fire signs (Aries, Leo, Sagittarius): azurite, larimar
Water signs (Cancer, Scorpio, Pisces): aquamarine, blue lace
     agate
Earth signs (Taurus, Virgo, Capricorn): amazonite, chrysocolla

To balance emotions, offer comfort and protection, and enhance all relationships, wear these pendants over the heart:

Air signs (Gemini, Libra, Aquarius): pink calcite, rose quartz
Fire signs (Aries, Leo, Sagittarius): malachite, emerald
Water signs (Cancer, Scorpio, Pisces): green tourmaline,
     prehnite
Earth signs (Taurus, Virgo, Capricorn): green jade, epidote

CRYSTAL MAGIC: IT'S IN THE BAG

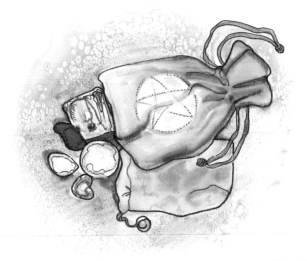

If you prefer to carry your stones rather than wear them, place them in a mojo or charm bag so they don't get jostled about or lost. Keeping multiple stones together will also foster a bond between them, blending their energies to increase their impact. Thus, it is important to pair crystals that complement each other; you wouldn't include stones for boosting energy with ones for calming anxiety. For fragile stones, keep them solo rather than in a bag with others so they don't break; tuck them into a pocket, or keep them in a desk or on a nightstand and hold for a few minutes each day.

Create Your Own Crystal Charm Bag

Pick a bag in the color that corresponds with your desires, and choose crystals that support those intentions. Assemble it on the day of the week named for the planet that governs your goal.

COLOR	PLANET	DAY	GOAL
Black	Saturn	Saturday	Banishing, Binding, Protection, Wisdom
Blue	Jupiter	Thursday	Career, Finances, Influence, Success
Brown	Earth	All	Healing, Grounding, Animal Protection
Green	Venus	Friday	Fertility, Love, Luxury, Prosperity, Rejuvenation
Gold	Sun	Sunday	Abundance, Growth, Healing, God Energy
Orange	Mercury	Wednesday	Communication, Fast Luck, Mind, Rapid Recovery
Pink	Venus	Friday	Friendship, Love, Self-Care, Feminine Energy
Purple	Mercury	Wednesday	Astral Travel, Divination, Sovereignty
Red	Mars	Tuesday	Courage, Strength, Sex, Vitality, Masculine Energy
Silver	Moon	Monday	Psychic Ability, Dream Work, Goddess Energy
White	Moon	Monday	Intuition, Purification, General Blessings
Yellow	Sun	Sunday	Cash Flow, Lavishness, New Beginnings, Healing

ACTIVATING YOUR CHARM BAG

- Sit in a comfortable position in a place where you will not be disturbed.

- Close your eyes and breathe deeply, letting go of any mundane thoughts. When you feel relaxed and focused, open your eyes.

- Place the crystals in your dominant hand or on a charging plate.

- Think of the goal you want them to help you accomplish. Visualize what it would look like if your dreams came to be, or write it down.

- Place the crystals into the charm bag; you may add dried herbs, small metal charms, or other tokens that coincide with your purpose.

- Anoint the charm bag (place 2–3 drops onto it) with an essential or blended magical oil to feed it.

- Periodically hold the bag or acknowledge it throughout the day.

If you are new to working with crystals, a **clear quartz** is an excellent choice. It also makes a good "leader" stone that you can work with first in any meditation or intention session. It will enhance your own psychic ability and pave the way for any other stones you add. When carried daily, it will amplify your intentions to the Universe.

Attracting and Manifesting on the Go

One of the most common reasons people carry crystals with them is to attract or manifest something (or someone). To put the magic into your daily grind, these are the primary stones that we recommend to our clients:

Our Favorite Tumbled Stones for Manifesting Abundance and Money

A sunny attitude attracts abundance, and **citrine** is like a drop of sunshine. Place a citrine in a pocket or wallet to invite in wealth and success. Always bring one along if you're seeking or starting a new job; it opens doors and builds a positive attitude for every day.

Pyrite is our go-to for summoning more bling into anyone's life, and its golden color lends it special influence if you need better luck with your finances. Leanne wears a pyrite ring on her left hand to bring in the Benjamins while gambling, and Sandra has a pyrite Sun disk pendant she picked up in Florida—the Sunshine State—for whenever she wants to manifest luxury and abundance.

Our friend Vinnie always carries an **aventurine** in his left pocket, which helps him get more tips at work. Aventurine reinforces leadership abilities and determination, and attracts abundance and affluence.

Sandra keeps a **malachite** in her coin purse, which has traveled with her since her first teacher, Richard Ravish, told her that if she kept a malachite with her money, she would never lack it. The stone is shaped like the head of a dragon, which is her first power animal, and while she has hundreds of stones, it is one of her favorites.

OUR FAVORITE TUMBLED STONES FOR MANIFESTING LOVE AND POSITIVE RELATIONSHIPS

When it comes to love, **rose quartz** is the quintessential pocket companion. It is a magnet for romance, yes, but it also excels at promoting self-love, which is the key to all healthy relationships. Call on it when you need affection, friendship, and compassion, or to soften negativity in tense situations. Keep it close on second dates (when you know you're interested) and for all manner of romantic encounters.

If you're healing a wounded heart, **rhodonite** is one of the best stones you could choose to move on and repair trust issues to avoid self-sabotage in new relationships. The telltale combination of pink and black sets it apart from other love-related stones, and visually reminds you to accept both the light and dark of the past and learn from experience without losing hope for the future.

If you're looking for a love that can meet you on all levels, add **rhodochrosite** to your roster. It awakens passion and desire to the body, mind, and soul, and keeps the blues at bay.

Whether you're dealing with a lover, friend, or coworker, strong communication is the basis for every healthy relationship—especially when all three are the same person. **Lapis lazuli** will help you choose words that are compassionate and honest. When communication with people at a distance is a particular struggle, place a lapis near your phone (or computer if you're chatting online). This will aid in perceiving a person's true intent.

As we discussed, **malachite** works wonders for finances, and it is also a welcome addition to your charm bag when your goal is to improve your relationships, as it can open up even the most bitter heart. This healing stone is basically the mineral equivalent of a couple's therapist that you can carry all day long.

For more recommendations for stones to carry in charm bags, see the glossary.

CRYSTALS ON THE ROAD

We all need protection when traveling to new places, and crystal lovers never leave home without backup. Whether it is the physical act of hopping on a plane or just stepping outside your personal comfort zone, traveling can be scary, and the right stone can tone down the anxiety of any trip. Without that stress, you can focus on the pleasure and excitement of a new place and perspective. We both absolutely love to hit the road and are happy to share our top travel companions.

TRAVEL BY LAND

Driving in unfamiliar territory can cause fear and trepidation in even confident travelers. Crystals can bring confidence, awareness, and safety to any road trip when placed around the car to protect the vehicle and its occupants: the trunk, the glove compartment, under seats, on the dashboard, even dangling from a keychain.

Many of our days are spent commuting in cars, not driving on a fun adventure. It is vital to keep the atmosphere of your vehicle pleasant, protective, and free from negative energies. Before you bring in crystals, clean your car, which will banish bad mojo. In short, get rid of the garbage, both psychic and physical. We don't want to add beautiful treasures from the earth to a pile of old coffee cups and wrappers; it simply will not be as effective. Clear the air with frankincense and myrrh, or a similar cleansing smoke of your choice. Once the car is washed and decluttered, the crystals can enter.

For as long as she has been behind the wheel, Leanne has always been a nervous driver. These days, she keeps an **amethyst** and a

hematite under her driver's seat to ease her fear. Amethyst's vibration helps the car run smoothly and it helps her drive effortlessly, and hematite is protective and grounding, so it keeps her focus on the road. It also enhances mindfulness during traffic, aiding in preventing accidents and keeping her from getting lost.

Other crystals that take the crazy out of driving:

Selenite protects both cars and passengers, so place the stone in the center console for defense against crashes and malfunction. Selenite also makes family road trips more pleasant by defusing frustrations and clearing the way for communication. There's nothing like a road trip to generate deep discussions, so make sure you're setting the right mood to take advantage!

Citrine keeps drivers vigilant. Place the crystal in a cup holder, preferably near your to-go cup of coffee or tea. It offers clarity and a positive attitude while on the road. Zap that road rage away.

TRAVEL BY AIR

Traveling expands the mind and feeds the soul. Seeing the globe and experiencing different cultures can change your worldview and enrich your world. Air is the element most associated with intellect, logic, reason, and communication, and air travel is often the fastest way to get where you want to be; but as we all know, it can be a hectic hassle. Here are our suggestions to make air travel a breeze:

Tuck a **malachite** into your purse and another into each piece of your luggage to tamp down the confusing chaos of travel and protect against mishaps.

Sandra swears by **blue calcite** to calm even the most anxious plane passengers, keep the vibes chill, and bring an aura of positivity. It even looks like a beautiful blue sky.

Air travel often means passing your body and belongings through X-ray machines. **Shungite** removes residual electromagnetic energy, keeping you and your items clear.

Bring a **moonstone** on your next flight, especially if you will be crossing bodies of water. As it keeps your path free from traffic and delays, you'll feel its soothing effects and let go of any rage or frustration.

TRAVEL BY SEA

There is something magical and humbling about traveling on the water. It can be both awe-inspiring and terrifying. When a person travels by water, they are surrounded by the element most associated with depth of emotion, so unsurprisingly, it is often a bonding experience when traveling with someone else. Each type of body of water has its own energy: Rivers contain the grace of going with the flow. Lakes have a calm, mysterious spirit. The sea is endless in its wild beauty and majesty, changing without warning—a ship can start out sailing at ease, but before long, the calm rocking can turn turbulent, with mighty waves swelling to terrifying heights.

Leanne is a frequent cruiser. She loves the endless views of the ocean meeting the sky on the horizon. Sandra prefers a quick turn around the bay rather than long trips in open water. Either way, we both love the salt air and the sound of the surf against the ship, and we always have our crystal jewelry and tumbled stones with us when we are heading out on the water.

Jasper brings balance to body and spirit and provides relief for motion sickness on land, in air, and at sea. Make sure to pack jasper before cruising to reduce hassle and angst. The stone will also reduce frustrations between travel companions—handy when you're stuck on a ship together for an extended period. Jasper's nourishing and rejuvenating energy lends luck and good fortune to the seabound voyager. As you know by now, there are a number of kinds of jasper, but the obvious choice here is **ocean jasper**. It is associated with balance due to its origin story, about the combination of fire (hot lava) and water (cooling liquid), so it is a prime choice to sustain your sea legs.

Another no-brainer is **aquamarine**, once considered the treasure of mermaids and a good luck charm for sailors. Some people believe the crystal is exceptionally strong when submerged in water. Leanne's fellow cruisers have placed an aquamarine in a glass of water on the nightstand in their cabin for courage and protection. The stone soothes anxiety and brings luck to those traveling over water, and can calm sea sickness and create unexpected positive adventures. Romans often offered aquamarine to the god Neptune, so carry it when you're heading to His domain to curry favor in the form of calm seas and kind winds.

4

HARMONY, PEACE, AND COOPERATION: CRYSTALS IN THE LIVING ROOM

The living room, also called the great room, is the family commons and the traditional space for entertaining guests. As the primary shared space in the home, it is also where memories are made and bonding takes place, so it should ideally be free of negative energy and bickering. Couples discuss current events or the events of their days there, or just cuddle on the couch. Introverts chill in their favorite chair with a cup of tea and a cozy blanket. Families can carry on traditions from previous generations with playing card and board games. In short, it's the ideal location to work with crystals that foster harmony, peace, and cooperation.

THE LIVING ROOM SHOULD RADIATE COMFORT, NOT ELECTROMAGNETIC FIELDS

Since we often keep electronics like televisions, stereo and gaming systems, and computers in the living room, it is also one of the top spots in the home for low-level electric and magnetic field exposure, which some people report causes disturbances in sleep, mood, and concentration; headaches; and even ringing in the ears or vision problems. To nullify those negative impacts, stones like **smoky quartz**, **black tourmaline**, and **shungite** should be placed near any electronics to absorb their energy. Spheres will disperse their protective energy throughout the entire room and create a bubble of defense against the frequencies, or you could pick a tower to stand guard.

All Together Now

Cocktail parties and celebrations of all kinds are frequently hosted in the great room. If you experience anxiety and stress when attending social gatherings, that's normal. It's not always easy blending friends from different backgrounds, and it might be hard to imagine your cubicle mate connecting with your high school bestie. In those cases, use crystal energy to promote tranquillity and mutual respect. Place tumbled **aquamarine** and **chrysocolla** stones around the space to stimulate conversation and help your guests get to know one another. Aquamarine will lend social confidence to introverts and allow them to open up, and chrysocolla assists in listening with an open mind to new points of view.

When it comes to holiday or birthday gatherings, when family members who may not see eye to eye are forced to share space together, we recommend **citrine**, which radiates the joyful power of the Sun. Citrine smooths over conflicts, leading to greater communication and understanding, and can even tamp down sibling rivalry. Leanne places tumbled citrine and rose quartz crystals under her couch cushions during gatherings to ensure a good time is had by all.

When the ones we love are intolerant in one way or another— which unfortunately many of us have experienced—turn to **chrysoprase** to dissipate those unpleasant behaviors and change closed-minded and stubborn people's energy. Activate its detoxifying power prior to a social gathering by holding it in your hands and taking a few deep breaths, then walking around the space with it in your dominant hand. If you have a wand or tower, aim it at the outer walls of the room; if it's a sphere, visualize a bubble of energy clearing the space and filling it with a relaxed, welcoming vibe.

When arguments break out, **rhodonite** opens the door to forgiveness, stabilizes fractured relationships, brings us together in harmony and understanding, banishes disappointment, and supports compassion. As it opens up the heart and center of love, it heals old wounds, too. Place a rhodonite tower, pyramid, or sphere in the living room to bring its power to those who need to mend fences and move on to joy.

Sometimes a bad day at work gets tracked into the home like mud on your shoes. On those evenings, banish the bullshit and bring in some sanity protection with **black tourmaline**, which not only shields the occupants of any room from the echoes of the chaos but focuses us on the present moment to pay attention to the people who matter the most. Black tourmaline can also help bring back balance for those who are overly influenced by the onslaught of negativity from social media and internet sites. It works particularly well in combination with **red jasper**, especially when life has thrown your family a curve ball. Red jasper's encouraging, revitalizing sensibility is beneficial if you feel overwhelmed, particularly if you are experiencing fallout from things that are out of your control. It can also be helpful for anyone who has experienced emotional trauma from a bad relationship: Place it in the room, and hold it when you need support.

PARTY PREGAMING WITH CRYSTALS

A crystal meditation before any gathering will empower you to dictate the energy flow in your home and start the party off on the right foot. An hour before guests arrive, infuse your body and your space with positive energy. Choose the crystal (or crystals) that best represents the feeling you want to promote among the group. Sit in a comfortable place in your living room and hold the crystal(s) between your hands at chest height, or if this is not comfortable, place it in your lap or directly in front of you. Take a deep breath for each person you have invited, picturing them or saying their name out loud. Envision the power of the stone enveloping them. For instance, if you are holding a rose quartz, imagine them smiling, bathed in pink light. When you have done this for each guest, tuck the crystal into the centerpiece; if using more than one, place them around the room so they fill the space with merry vibes for the whole event.

MOVIE NIGHT MINERALS

Movie nights are a beloved tradition in many households. When gathering in the living room to watch something together, **rose quartz** should be a staple. Rose quartz vibrates support and love and promotes an affectionate atmosphere. Its nurturing nature cultivates serenity in any casual hang. Place a rose quartz sphere on the coffee table with **blue calcite** to bring an undercurrent of peace to the room. Know a chatterbox who gets overly excited and talks through movie dialogue? **Hematite** will ground even the most wired watchers (and generally reduces day-to-day tensions, allowing for a more fulfilling family time). It also brings greater focus and concentration to the group, so even loved ones who have issues paying attention will be absorbed in enjoying the common experience. Another lesser-known benefit: It curbs couch snacking! Leanne often carries tumbled hematite in her bra to limit trips to the refrigerator or cabinet when marathoning her favorite shows.

NETFLIX AND CHILL

As fun as it is to hit the town for a date, a quiet night on the sofa can be pure heaven. Heighten the spirit of laid-back romance with crystal energy. While most people think of rose quartz when it comes to a love connection, don't sleep on **kunzite**, the MVP when you are first inviting a romantic interest over to hang. It will turn the volume up on your confidence and charisma so that no matter what's on the TV, you will be the most interesting thing to watch. If it is too soon for the bedroom—or you're hoping that it will progress to that more intimate space over the course of the evening—start off in the living room. Before your guest arrives, place **fluorite** on the coffee table, or wherever conversations will take place, to reduce nervousness and invite in understanding, allowing the energy to flow effortlessly between you two. Another stone to bring in during the "honeymoon" stage of dating is **malachite**, which can heal the wounds of the past, paving the way for a fresh start.

If you are in a long-standing relationship, strengthen your bond by bringing in **amazonite**, which disperses bad moods and alleviates the mundane pressures of life that can weigh heavily on our minds. It also opens up the heart and throat, encouraging loving communication, and aids lovers in finding the right words, giving a voice to the heart. In ancient Rome, **lapis lazuli** was believed to honor the goddess of love, Venus; and when having a heart-to-heart conversation with a romantic partner, it promotes active listening. A freeform altar stone blends in nicely, and a few tumbled stones in the corners of the room also raise its vibrations to make the living room a more loving room.

It's All Fun and Games

When choosing crystals to influence a living room, make sure to focus on pleasure and happiness. A room that radiates togetherness will motivate even the most aloof teenager to join in on family activities—at least some of the time. **Carnelian's** warm confidence boosts feelings of fun and will get everyone involved on game night, turning moments into memories. For social and emotional ease among family or friends, a beautiful blue sphere of **apatite** will bring a glow of contentment to the space. It also fosters inner peace and clarity, so it makes for a more exciting game-time experience; in training and school settings, it is used to expand knowledge and wisdom, so consider brain-teaser, thinking-cap, or problem-solving games. And even though apatite might get us feeling extra confident, it also keeps us humble with its down-to-earth vibe, so we can cheer each other on and better enjoy each other's company.

Leanne's living room often turns into a competitive place, where video games are played and digital "wars" are won and lost. (Without putting too fine a point on it, the generally harmonious space turns into the Hunger Games, and battle cries like "May the odds be ever in your favor" can be heard throughout the house.) Friendly competition quickly can become a clash, with players going from laughing together to cussing each other out faster than you can say "game over." Leanne places **pink calcite** around the living room to lighten even the most uptight gamer, dissolving disputes and transforming confrontation into cooperation.

Some of us shut down altogether at the thought of group activities, and crystal encouragement can assist in bringing the family together in one space. **Garnet**'s assertive energy will bolster the confidence of folks who are timid and reluctant in crowds, as this unmistakable deep-red powerhouse assists in finding inner strength. A garnet sphere in a central location, or a few tumbled stones close to the action, creates a dynamic ambience that supports and rewards recreational risk-taking.

FRIENDS AND FAMILY ACTIVITY: TENDING A CRYSTAL SPHERE GARDEN

A collection of spheres on a living room shelf is both beautiful and useful: The spheres passively set the tone and even generate a desired atmosphere, but they can also be held and passed around the room to activate and empower them further. Try associating a keyword with each sphere in your garden. When family or friends gather, take turns choosing one to pass around and talk about what you think of when you hear the keyword, or something that has happened in the past week that relates to it. For instance, if the keyword for a **rose quartz** sphere is *love*, each person may share a recent experience in which they expressed or received love. If the keyword for **sodalite** is *cooperation*, they may relate a story in which they themselves or someone they know helped someone in need. As time goes on, the spheres may take on multiple keywords, each holding positive memories. See the glossary on page 187 for keyword ideas.

SANDRA'S LIVING ROOM SPHERE GARDEN

These are the stones that make up Sandra's sphere garden, in order from smallest to largest:

Larvikite—"Patience is a virtue," Sandra's grandfather used to say, and larvikite is crucial because it cultivates patience, creativity, and follow-through.

Banded brown aragonite—the crystal equivalent of putting your bare feet on the cool ground. Sandra is a city Witch, but her love of nature runs deep, and this sphere connects her with Mother Earth.

Ruby kyanite—this combination of minerals supports a balance of dynamic and peaceful energies, so Sandra can remain cool, calm, and collected, even in the craziness and chaos of everyday life.

Carnelian—Sandra places this longtime favorite throughout the house, but in the living room, it acts like a battery, keeping her physical energy up as she tackles whatever the day brings.

Labradorite—because this stone is like a megaphone into the spirit world, Sandra places it anywhere she wants to be connected to her loved ones on the other side. Her living room once belonged to her grandparents, where her nana used to sit by the front window to pray the rosary; so this room has held an aura of spiritual energy for many decades.

Garnet—like carnelian, garnet boosts physical energy. It also ignites passion in every sense, so it adds some spice when the days are feeling a bit dull. It is a powerful stone for artists and creatives of all types, so it is a must-have for any author, vocalist, poet, or writer.

Rainbow moonstone—part of Sandra's spiritual work over the past twenty years has been hosting a rite called Death and Rebirth: Ritual Transformation, and rainbow moonstone is her go-to for facilitating change, creating new pathways, starting fresh, and manifesting dreams. She has kept some form of this stone around for decades, and this sphere is the single largest piece in her considerable collection.

Black moonstone—this form of moonstone is particularly linked with the Moon Goddess in Her Crone aspect, and it symbolizes Her wisdom. It shreds any negativity in its domain, transmuting it to fuel for more badassery. This is one of Sandra's absolute favorite spheres; she has more black moonstone spheres than any others. When she needs to call upon the wisdom of the ancients, this is the sphere she reaches for, and it is a welcome presence in the room where she often gathers to discuss topics with her coven.

Selenite—this large white orb seems to glow in the light of the lamp above it. Its main purpose is to cleanse and clear the energy of the rest of the sphere garden and the room as a whole.

Golden sheen obsidian—this sphere has the most sentimental value, as it once belonged to Sandra's friend Shawn Poirier, who passed away in 2007. Golden sheen obsidian allows us to face our deepest fears, and since Shawn was the first Witch in our friend group to make the journey to the other side, he is also the first among us to face that fear we all share. This particular sphere is also a classic choice for scrying. Sandra has consulted it on many occasions, and its former owner has been known to weigh in from spirit.

Clear quartz—Sandra's beloved traditional clear quartz crystal ball has a prominent place in the main room, raising the vibrations of the entire house. It amplifies the power of the sphere garden and helps the stones act in harmony with one another. This mega sphere can be seen on the episode of *The Real Housewives of New York City* titled "The Witching Hour" as the centerpiece of the séance, which allowed spirit to come through loud and clear. Its incredibly high vibrations achieved what many viewers believed impossible: None of the cast members fought while in its presence!

5

HEALTH AND PERSONAL ENERGY: CRYSTALS IN THE KITCHEN

The kitchen is the heart of any home, where our literal nourishment is stored and prepared. While it is still a place of utility, in our modern houses, it is also a place of luxury, no longer tucked away in the cellar or an efficiency galley. In the past few generations, we have come to understand the real value and power of the kitchen (and been relieved of much strenuous labor by advances in technology). It is more than a place to make a meal. Friends and family gather there not only to cook but to connect. It is where we link up with our partners after a day of work, where we share stories of our day and seek comfort from both the food and the fellowship. It is where we feed our appetites *and* our souls. For that reason, it is a welcoming site for crystals and stones.

KITCHEN AS TEMPLE: MONUMENTAL MAGIC

In recent years, natural stone has been trending in kitchen design, but we can trace the roots of using many of these materials back over centuries. When you think about ancient monuments to the Old Gods, you probably think of **marble** and **granite**. Marble is a form of calcite, meaning that the crystals interlock and create the durable material that holds up many famous buildings that are still standing today, like the Taj Mahal in India. Granite is rich in quartz and feldspar, two of the most popular crystals found in metaphysical shops around the world. The exterior of the Red Pyramid of Egypt includes granite, and the Great Pyramid contains a granite sarcophagus. So many places of power incorporate these stones; it makes sense that yours would, too.

These epic stones can both beautify and empower the kitchen, and you may already come into contact with one or both of them every day. A stone as cool to the touch as marble can take the heat out of any situation. Placing your palms on it and taking a few deep breaths can help you take a step back from an emotional situation to regain your composure.

The legendarily hard and durable granite, also commonly found in modern kitchens, contains powerful protection energy, so these countertops are beautiful, practical, *and* magical. Granite is millions of years old, as old as any material on the planet. It is made of cooled magma, the molten lava at the core of the earth. Most homeowners choose granite countertops because they are practical: heat-resistant and difficult to damage. So it's no surprise to learn that granite is associated with self-defense. In fêng shui (the Chinese philosophical practice of designing our living spaces to be in harmony with the natural world), placing granite in the center of the room—like as an island countertop—promotes good health, grounds chaotic energy, and disperses negativity. It aids in constructive communication and supports positive group gatherings, so it's a must-have for the kitchen. If you want to bring granite into your kitchen but remodeling is out of your budget, choose a granite mortar and pestle to grind roots and herbs, a trivet, or a larger cheese, challah, or cutting board.

FOOD AND SPIRITS

Including granite where you prepare food opens up the mind to possibilities. Since it helps people communicate, it can lead to a more positive outcome for gatherings of families and friends. No wonder it's such a popular choice! **Labradorite** is one form of granite known for its particularly hard surface, and it's especially popular in bar tops due to its translucent nature: It can be backlit for an incredible visual effect, as its iridescent flashes shift and change when viewed from different angles.

Witches know labradorite as spectrolite, a name it earned due to its ability to enhance communication with those who have crossed over and amplify the voice of spirit. It is often found in jewelry and worn by mediums to connect us to our ancestors. This is another reason it is an appropriate stone for the kitchen: The kitchen contains so many family memories. Think about all the recipes you learned from your parents or grandparents, the dishes they were proudest to serve to loved ones, the dishes that friends requested for potlucks. Those recipes are a conduit to people who have crossed over into spirit. Preparing them simultaneously transports you back in time and carries those traditions into future generations. While making them for those you love, connect with your ancestors by placing a labradorite near the stove. We both keep a labradorite in our kitchens to feel the spirit of our grandmothers when we re-create their recipes. (When Leanne dreams of her grandmothers, they are nearly always in the kitchen; and Sandra's kitchen actually was her grandmother's at one time, so her energy is ever-present.)

Travertine is another countertop or floor option with metaphysical clout. The sunny stone brightens up both the kitchen and its occupants, promoting healing and clarity of thought while neutralizing any negative energies entering your home. Sitting in the breakfast nook with travertine elements, conversations flow easily, and children benefit from a boost in confidence and a positive outlook. **If you have a travertine floor, try focusing on pulling bright, happy vibes up through your feet as you stir a pot on the stovetop. The happiness and peace of mind you feel will be transferred into the food you make.**

In the preparation of a meal, cleansing any metaphysical toxins from the food is important for health of body and mind. A **clear quartz crystal** point, a must-have for any kitchen, directs discord away with its unpolluted and pure aura. When dining with young children, it can also impart knowledge from great-grandparents and other ancestors in spirit. It intensifies our ability to listen and comprehend, which is a welcome addition to any gathering of the tribe. **Place a crystal cluster or tower on a counter or as part of a centerpiece to invite balance and harmony into family dinners. Even the crankiest in-laws or angstiest teen cannot resist its rainbowblasting power.**

Kiss the Cook:
Love in the Kitchen

We gather to eat for all sorts of reasons. Sometimes we want to fix the past and reconnect over a meal. When our romantic relationships are strained, we want to sit down to talk things out. Eating together is a sacred act. Simply breaking bread opens doors for love, peace, and friendship to come in.

The most well-known stone for encouraging all forms of love is **rose quartz**, which has been revered for centuries for its ability to magnify the powers of beauty and intimacy. Watch any home renovation show and you'll hear the host talk about quartz countertops. Clear quartz is more common, but rose quartz is a true showstopper. You don't have to install an entire countertop to bring the rose quartz's energy into the kitchen. Leanne hangs one over her stove to promote family bonding, and Sandra keeps one with a cache of stones in the bottom of a large candle holder in the center of her kitchen for harmonious communication.

Rose quartz doesn't just beautify a kitchen, it magically imbues it with what Witches playfully call "Pink Light." We've all heard that adage "The way to a man's heart is through his stomach." When you want someone to be sweet on you, bust out the rose quartz with the recipes and bring affection and tenderness into whatever you are mak-

HOW TO MAKE A SAFE CRYSTAL ELIXIR

Place a crystal in contact with water to create an elixir. Water takes on the energy of things that are placed into it, so only nontoxic crystals, such as clear quartz, rose quartz, and amethyst, should come into direct contact with any that you drink. (See page 91 for a list of crystals we have found to be water-safe.) If you are not sure if the stone you want to use to infuse is nontoxic, you can still make an effective elixir that contains its energy. There are a number of infusion products on the market, where crystals can be placed into an interior glass chamber that is sealed off from the water, or you can put a glass container of water into a bowl and surround the glass with the crystals whose power you wish to use to infuse. We recommend that the container remain undisturbed for three days and three nights. Place it in direct sunlight for infusions for growth, expansion, abundance, new beginnings, fertility, and happiness. Place it in moonlight for infusions pertaining to intuition, psychic power, or mediumship, as well as ridding yourself of unwanted energy, toxic relationships, bad habits, illness, or addictions. When you drink the crystal elixir, envision the energy of the stone revitalizing you. (If you have dropped crystals directly into the water, remove them prior to drinking it.) You may choose to say an affirmation to reinforce its purpose: Write it in your own words and speak it from the heart.

ing. You can infuse drinks and even cooking water with rose quartz by making a **crystal elixir** (see page 65 for instructions). Stop a lovers' spat in its tracks. Mend fences with a neighbor. Bring sexy back with your main squeeze. As they enjoy the meal you've made, envision them surrounded by the loving glow of the rose quartz. Bathe them in Pink Light in your mind's eye, and soon you will see them soften up, like butter.

VITAMINS AND MINERALS, LITERALLY

Food can heal us from the inside of our bodies to the depth of our spirits, and when we think of it that way, we see how important it is to check our mind-set about the food we eat and how we eat it. It is often said "The secret is in the sauce," and that is certainly true at Leanne's house. She adds a protective zap to her Sunday "gravy" with crystals as she cooks. Leanne says: *Wednesday may be spaghetti day, but Sunday is when my family traditionally serves macaroni and meatballs. Right next to my spoon rest, I keep a **sunstone** and a piece of **amber** to ensure that hungry family and friends gain the blessings of the Sun. While I wait for the pasta water to boil, I dip a cheesecloth bag with a **carnelian** and a **tiger's eye** inside it for strength, vitality, and grounding.*

The whole concept of "saying grace" stems from the idea that gratitude should be a part of the act of nourishment, and we can take this a step further by choosing foods that are associated with the things we want for ourselves, then amplify the power in those foods with stones and crystals to get closer to achieving our goals. To get you started, we have provided a number of recipes in the appendix that list not only edible ingredients and their associations but also which crystals and stones to pair with the meal for the best results. Think of it like choosing a wine to complement the meal.

Sandra says: *In my kitchen, I have always had houseplants, and at times culinary herbs, as part of the landscape. The light that comes through the windows in the afternoon is perfect for everything from growing a healthy pothos vine to a potted rosemary, and I always include a* **quartz crystal** *in the pot, charged up with the power of the Sun, to amplify growth and radiate positive energy to, and from, the spirits in the plants. I have also placed stones carved with words into a growing plant's pot and envisioned those wishes growing with the plant. Right now, I have a beautiful spider plant that has two stones nestled near its roots: one reads happiness, and the other, health. I figure if I've got those, I am a lucky woman indeed.*

You wash your fruits and veggies to cleanse them of dirt or chemicals, and you can also cleanse their energy, and the energy of the kitchen itself, with a few well-placed stones and crystals. The same way leaving an open box of baking soda in the fridge will pick up offensive smells, strategically placing your stones in your kitchen will keep the room free from offensive energy. **Black onyx, black kyanite,** and **nuummite** make a powerful trio, and you can place them into a small bowl made of wood, clay, or porcelain. Add a piece of **blue kyanite** to keep them clean and clear: It never requires cleansing, and actively safeguards other stones from accumulated negativity.

Amethyst is the chicken soup of the crystal world. It is one of our favorite healing stones, and it is one we love to infuse in our cooking water to imbue it with its power. Since the time of ancient Rome, amethyst has been used to break addictions; so bringing it into the kitchen can curb compulsive behaviors, such as overeating. It will also negate anxiety, fear, and stress that can lead to using food for comfort, and can help picky eaters warm up to trying new foods. Leanne has a client who puts amethyst on the dining room table to encourage her children to eat their vegetables and stop arguing.

Over the years, we have both been on a journey to greater wellness

WINDOWSILL MAGIC

One simple way to bring the family together is for each member to choose a stone to line up along the kitchen windowsill. Each stone should signify a blessing they wish for everyone in the home. (See the glossary on page 187 for a detailed list of stones and their metaphysical associations. Be careful with crystals in the window, as the prisms can focus heat and cause a fire. Choose a tumbled stone rather than a faceted one to avoid this issue.) After a family meal, have everyone add their stone to the windowsill and explain why they chose it. From that point on, the row of rocks will become a beautiful reminder of everyone's hopes and dreams for the family, and a lovely, loving way to connect with those positive feelings on difficult days.

(and weight loss), and amethyst has kept us focused on our goals. If you are struggling to lose weight, try keeping an amethyst and a piece of **white howlite** with you so you remember to make good choices and maintain your willpower.

Entertaining for a crowd can be stressful, especially when drama is on the guest list. Put that noise on block with **black tourmaline**, which acts as a powerful shield against negativity. If you keep black tourmaline on your windowsill or over your door, it will also ground the energy of those who enter so they can leave their daily strife behind. For an extra-powerful purge, place a black tourmaline in a glass filled with salt and a tablespoon of water. As the water evaporates, the energy of the tourmaline will be dispersed into the air, clearing it.

AN OUNCE OF PREVENTION

Just as food rich in vitamin C fights the common cold, crystals can provide the extra boost you need to ward off illness and disease. **Obsidian**, which is volcanic glass, is a cleanser and a protector. One particularly useful characteristic of obsidian is its ability to absorb electromagnetic radiation, a form of radiant energy that can affect a person's health after long-term exposure. One of the main sources of electromagnetic energy in the home is a frequent resident of the kitchen: the microwave. Place obsidian around your microwave as a shield against unwanted frequencies. As a bonus, obsidian will ground you and shield your aura. If you are hosting a gathering and know that some guests are bringing their emotional baggage, have obsidian on hand to protect everyone at the table.

Our kitchens should be welcoming and warm. The spirit of any room is cooperatively formed by everyone who uses it, so make your kitchen a place where people feel safe and loved. In every detail, from the fixtures to the foods, you can use the magic of crystals and stones to support health and wellness, cleanse negativity, and manifest the goals of each person who comes to the table.

6

REST, DREAMS, AND SEX: CRYSTALS IN THE BEDROOM

Our bedrooms are one of the most private places in our homes—in our lives, when you think about it. We may entertain guests there, but rarely do we invite outsiders into this space. This is a room that is set up for our comfort and our comfort only, and therefore, the magic that is done here is for our most intimate relationships. This is where we must be able to shed the worries of the day, connect with our partners, and replenish our bodies and minds through sleep. It is also where we can receive psychic information in the form of dreams.

CRYSTALS TO HELP YOU SLEEP LIKE A ROCK

Sleeping is a highly underrated, absolutely vital part of one's overall health. If a person does not get the proper amount of rest, their body will not be prepared and recharged for the next day. Any athlete will tell you that the three keys to success are practice/exercise, dietary choices/food intake, and good rest. Lack of sleep can cause brain fog, weight gain, illness, depression, and heart issues, among countless other problems, in a domino effect. Resting allows us to dream, and dreaming can grant us visions of the future as well as visits with people of our past. Crystals and stones can both encourage restful sleep and open the mind to the world of dreams.

Many people struggle with falling asleep and, more important, staying asleep. Insomnia impacts their lives both physically and emotionally. While the mind rests, the soul travels and the body heals. **Rainbow moonstone** sitting on a nightstand or tucked under a mattress can reduce emotional disturbances to allow for a more restful night. We personally wear, carry, or place moonstone on our nightstands to connect with, and receive protection from, the divine feminine. Its passive presence creates a serene space and even enhances lucid dreaming, which we will get into later in this chapter.

SOME OF THE OTHER SLEEP "ROCK STARS" IN OUR ENTOURAGE

Lepidolite—promotes happiness and helps combat anxiety and stress

Celestite—brings a sense of comfort and protection, connection to "guardian angels"

Blue calcite—has a deeply soothing, calming energy

Fluorite—clears the mind, quiets racing thoughts

Lapis lazuli—psychic-power enhancer for fruitful dreams, helps with pre-sleep meditation

BATTLING INSOMNIA

Nothing is worse after an overwhelming day than being unable to sleep, or waking up hours before the dreaded alarm goes off. If you struggle to fall asleep, or to return to sleep if you wake up in the middle of the night, you've probably already researched and tried these mundane tips; but in case you haven't, here are the steps commonly recommended to help with insomnia:

1. Set your body's rhythm: plan to go to bed and wake up at the same times every night/day.

2. Create a sleep routine that includes transition time from activity to rest.

3. Put electronic devices like your phone, tablet, or laptop away at least a half hour before lights out.

4. Finish any meals or snacks at least two hours before bedtime.

5. Limit your caffeine intake to the first eight hours you are awake each day.

If you've tried all that and are still having a hard time, it's time to enlist help from the mineral and plant kingdoms.

We both occasionally have issues sleeping; sometimes it is because we are busy and our minds don't want to shut off. For those evenings, Leanne keeps a piece of **amethyst** on her nightstand to quiet the intrusive thoughts in her head. Amethyst, or "nature's tranquilizer," relaxes and brings peace to a troubled mind, which makes it a go-to for psychic power as well as sleep. It promotes the body's natural healing response that is activated by restful sleep and maximizes the restorative energy only a good snooze can bring. Its herbal cousin is lavender, which is likewise associated with serenity and is commonly used in room or pillow/sheet sprays to help with relaxation. **Pair an amethyst tumbled or palm stone with lavender oil for a gentle slumber: Dab a small drop of oil on your fingers and rub it into the crystal.**

YOUR NEW BEDTIME CRYSTAL RITUAL

Once you are ready for bed—teeth brushed, phone off, with your usual nightly routine completed—hold an amethyst palm stone or wand in your hand while sitting on the edge of the bed. Close your eyes. Take nine long, slow breaths, inhaling intensely and exhaling deeply. Pay close attention to the sound of your breath. Then focus on feeling the energy of the amethyst pulsing in your hand, releasing any mundane thoughts of the day that may enter your mind. After the first nine breaths, resume your normal, relaxed breathing, and stay centered on the growing aura of the amethyst. Do this for as long as it feels comfortable. Start with 3–5 minutes while you are building the habit. When it feels right, place the amethyst under your pillow or on your bedside table, lie down, and allow rest to envelop you, like a warm blanket.

Place the amethyst on your forehead for a few minutes to relax tension and ease your mind toward sleep.

Sandra has a collection of stones in a wooden bowl on her nightstand, and using them in combination has proven to be the best cure for quieting down her racing mind: hematoid quartz, chrysanthemum stone, and fluorite. Each has been charged specifically for this purpose by a shard of blue kyanite that rests beside them in the bowl. Hematoid quartz contains hematite, which clears the head of excess worry. Chrysanthemum stone is prized for its abilities to rejuvenate and to cultivate inner peace. Fluorite is the crystal equivalent of a first responder when it comes to all things mental, so it works around the clock, while you're waking or sleeping, to protect, rescue, and maximize the mind's optimal state.

When Leanne wakes up in the middle of the night, she reaches for **howlite** and her journal and writes down all the thoughts stuck in her brain. **Howlite is a stress reliever and anger releaser, and many folks use it in meditation. It can also relieve insomnia when placed under a pillow.**

Leanne also suggests that before retiring for the evening, place **selenite** near your bed, which cleanses the overall energy and creates a grounding environment in any room. Its pure aura promotes sleep and invites harmony and peace into the bedroom. Sandra keeps selenite tealight holders in several rooms; the flame of the candle lights up the holder, creating a natural lamp that gives off comforting vibes. We highly recommend using one as a natural bedside light for your meditations, but be careful not to fall asleep with the candle burning. To be safe, meditate while sitting up in bed any time a candle is lit, and extinguish it prior to lying down.

SLEEPY-TEA UPGRADE

Drop a clean, tumbled **dalmatian jasper** stone into a pan of boiling water, give it a minute to steep, and then pour yourself a cup of chamomile tea with the infusion. This particular type of jasper is safe in water, absorbs negativity, and protects against nightmares, so you can rest easy. Chamomile is the go-to tea for peaceful sleep and is also known to keep nightmares at bay, so these two together are the literal dream team.

SLEEP CHARM BAG

Combine an **ammonite** stone (it is really a fossil!) for energetic protection and relaxation with star anise pods in a lavender-colored bag to banish negative thoughts and have a peaceful sleep. Hang near your bed or tuck into your pillowcase, and anoint it with lavender oil as part of your nightly routine.

GUARDIAN STONES FOR TRANQUILITY

A tower or sphere of **black tourmaline** will ground and calm a room while neutralizing any chaos. Place a tower or sphere of **selenite** alongside the tourmaline to cleanse and balance its energy and radiate tranquility to anyone snoozing in the room.

CRYSTAL VISIONS:
DREAMS

Dreams are the brain's way of knowing it exists. Dreaming helps us process spiritual, psychological, and physical trauma, and examining and interpreting dreams can help us come to terms with our emotions and resolve conflicts. In ancient Greece and Rome, dreams were seen as direct messages from the gods or the dead, and were even used to diagnose illnesses. The earliest known Greek writing on dreams is the fourth book of the Hippocratic treatise *On Regimen*, from the end of the fifth or beginning of the fourth century BCE. It is not a metaphysical work but rather a medical one. It outlines that dreams that were deemed "natural and true" could reveal information about bodily states and processes that were hidden from a physician's direct observation.

Most people believe they have no control of their dreams. But when pondered and interpreted, dreams are rich tools of self-discovery, revealing inner truths, exposing our shadow side, and bestowing messages and guidance. Unfortunately, many people cannot remember their dreams, so that wisdom gets lost as soon as they open their eyes. (Generally, you remember only the last dream you had before waking, despite experiencing a multitude throughout the night.) Stress, over-activity before bedtime, and, paradoxically, exhaustion can ruin sleep. In turn, over-tiredness impedes dream recall. This is not healthy for the psyche or the soul. A simple way to improve your sleep and dream experience is to work with crystals. Depending on the size and shape of the stones, they can be placed on a nightstand, tucked into a pillowcase, or slipped between the mattress and box spring.

Smoky quartz is an excellent stone for grounding and relaxation. Think of it as the crystal equivalent of a dream catcher: It banishes fearful feelings in your waking hours, and in nightmares while you doze. Keep it near your bed to prepare your brain for dreamtime. Its light grounding energy can help you sink into a deeper sleep while protecting your peace of mind. It can also help you hang on to the relevant information you receive in your dreams, so hold it in your nondominant hand for a few minutes before you sleep, and specifically concentrate on its abilities to activate them.

OUR DREAM RECALL COMBO

Place a smoky quartz, fluorite, and a Herkimer diamond in a lavender or light-blue charm bag. Dab vanilla essential oil—which boosts memory—onto the bag and your wrists. Tuck the charm into your pillowcase or hang it on your bedpost. Keep a dream diary on the nightstand with a pen/pencil handy so you can write down your dreams upon waking.

PROPHETIC DREAMS CHARM BAG

Place three bay leaves with an amethyst and a citrine (tumbled or faceted) into a deep-purple charm bag. Anoint it with essential lavender or mugwort oil, or one specially formulated with a mix of appropriate ingredients, like Pentagram Shoppe's Sleep & Dreams Magickal Oil, and hang it above your bed or tuck it into your pillowcase to divine the future through your dreams.

THE DARK SIDE OF THE MOON: NIGHTMARES

Nightmares cause sleepless nights for many of our clients. In fact, about half of the dream-related questions we get have to do with nightmares and how to stop them from ruining people's sleep and even damaging their waking world. These unwanted experiences can come from processing bad encounters from previous days, the foods we eat, or the negativity that permeates our consciousness.

Some nightmares are hyperrealistic, causing you to jolt awake with your heart racing. These terrifying episodes may keep you awake for an extended period of time, affecting your health and emotional stability. And the worst part is that sometimes, they become recurring, haunting you on multiple nights. So what can you do to eliminate them, or at least reduce their frequency and intensity?

First, protect yourself and those who share your bedroom from damaging influences. Negative energies will incite the mind to develop bad dreams. Creating a dream satchel will banish nightmares and manifest a peaceful night's sleep. Fill a white charm bag with a tumbled tiger's eye for strength and courage, a smoky quartz for grounding, and a black tourmaline and anise seeds for protection. Anoint the outside of the bag with 3 drops of rosemary oil, which is used to prevent evil spirits from haunting people who are at rest.

Hang it over the bed, and make sure to anoint it once a week to keep it active (Monday or Saturday nights would be good choices). Once you have protected yourself, you can feel better about exploring the messages the nightmares may contain, especially those that keep repeating. **In this case, placing a green jade under your pillow will help you understand the purpose and meaning of a nightmare. Green jade has been called a "dream stone," used for centuries to interpret the significance of the visions people carried from sleep into the waking world, good or bad.** Another choice is a **dream quartz,** which is a quartz crystal that contains epidote, another helpful stone when it comes to effectively and safely exploring the reasons behind bad dreams. Once the mystery is solved, the nightmares cease. Sandra says:

I had a number of scary dreams that started out harmless and turned apocalyptic, and I could not shake the feeling of impending doom in the days that followed. Working with epidote helped me unpack what was actually behind them: concerns about my mother's health, and decisions that would need to be made to make sure she was safe and able to remain as independent as possible until that was no longer an option. We were not on the brink of a war, the way my dreams appeared. The "bombs" that were dropping were heavy realizations about my mother's situation and my responsibilities as her caretaker. When I processed the true meaning of the battle in my nightmares, they stopped.

FROM PASSENGER TO DRIVER: LUCID DREAMING

Lucid dreaming is a form of metacognition, or awareness of your awareness; in this case, awareness that you are asleep. It often lets you control what happens in your dream, too, allowing you to explore the dream world, and/or your innermost self, without fear.

In a lucid dream, a person can do anything they have ever imagined. Flying? No problem! Breathing underwater? Check! However, it can be used for so much more.

You may find that you are able to control who appears in your dreams, providing an opportunity to work through relationship issues, retracing traumas and processing them with more positive outcomes, which can alleviate emotional damage from the past. To begin your lucid dreaming journey, try one or both of the following:

DREAM MAGIC TEA

Drop a clean, tumbled **apatite** stone into a teapot of boiling water, adding a teaspoon of blue vervain into the pot. Wait three minutes, and then pour yourself a cup of decaffeinated tea. Apatite aids in lucid dreaming, astral travel, and past-life discovery, and blue vervain is an herb that supports psychic visions and prophecy. Drink a cup before bed to unlock your abilities while you drowse.

DREAMWORKS CHARM BAG

Place a teaspoon of blue vervain and a pinch of mugwort with a **moonstone** (tumbled or faceted) into a silver charm bag. Anoint it with one of the essential oils listed in the appendix for dreams, and hang it above your bed or tuck it into your pillowcase to help you work on lucid or past-life dreaming or astral travel.

DREAM VISITS

Because of its liminal nature, dreamtime is the best time to open yourself up to psychic messages, particularly missives from those who have crossed over. Our connection to the spirit world is strongest when our rational mind is less active and our psychic mind comes up to the surface. Our loved ones can often reach us more easily in our dreamworld than our waking one, as the strict rules of reality bend, or fall away completely. Your strongest crystal ally in spirit communication will be **labradorite**, which acts like a megaphone into the Great Beyond, carrying your voice to your beloved dead while opening up a channel to receive messages in response.

A client came in heartbroken because she had not received a "visit" from her father, who had recently died. Her siblings had all seen him in their dreams. Leanne advised her to place a tumbled labradorite and dried rosemary into a black charm bag to facilitate a connection with her father's spirit. Weeks later the client returned, thrilled because she had finally had a dream about her dad hugging her; this brought her tremendous peace. Rosemary helps us remember our dreams. It specifically encourages dreaming of the dead. To invite your loved ones in spirit for a nighttime visit, anoint your pillowcase with a bit of rosemary oil and wear a piece of labradorite jewelry to sleep.

Roll Out the Dream Spirit Welcome Mat

Before sleeping, burn mugwort in the bedroom. You can light a bit of self-igniting charcoal and sprinkle dried mugwort on it. (Alternatively, you could anoint a candle with mugwort oil, or rub a bit between your palms and then clasp your hands over your nose and mouth and inhale.) With the scent in the air, hold a **labradorite** in your dominant hand and an **iolite** (if you don't have one, use **amethyst** or **clear/dream quartz**) in the other. Close your eyes, and breathe in the mugwort (be careful not to overdo it, as mugwort can be an irritant). The combination of the herb and stones opens your third eye to aid in everything from astral travel to spirit communication. If you wish to communicate with angels or your higher self, hold an **angelite** or **celestite** in place of the labradorite. Speak from the heart about your desire, saying either out loud or in your mind, "I open myself up to communicate with _____, and I welcome you to join me in my dreams tonight." Remember to keep your dream diary close to record any visits or messages.

MAKING THE EARTH MOVE: BEDROOM-MAGIC CRYSTALS

The bedroom is a place for love, affection, and communication. Intimacy is more than sex, of course. It is talking, laughing, and sharing your most vulnerable self with the person you love. (But sex can be damned important, too.) Working with crystals in the bedroom will help break down barriers that impede closeness and desire.

Rose quartz is one of the most popular love crystals, with good reason. Known as the "romance stone," it helps people who struggle with intimacy, its serene energy allowing heart healing and trust to take hold. **Just handling a rose quartz, you can feel its loving and peaceful energy, like an astral hug. Holding or wearing it eases tension and anger, and fosters understanding and compassion.** When having a dispute with a romantic partner, rose quartz cultivates forgiveness. For those sleeping alone, it promotes self-love and self-care for the happily single, heals heartache for those nursing the wounds of a bad breakup, and assists in finding new love when ready—but that is just the start of the loving harmony this crystal can deliver. Holding a rose quartz during a heated discussion with your partner can foster resolution so you can get back to holding each other. Bonus if it's shaped like a heart!

It's not uncommon for individuals or couples to suffer from anxiety regarding sex. Crystals enable us to break down the walls that are built due to tension, angst, and the drudgery of everyday life. Other people feel they have fallen into a slump, and they want to spice up their experience. Crystals can open you up to fresh ideas and help you reclaim your sexual power if it has gone by the wayside.

If you're feeling blocked from intensity and joy in your sex life, **red carnelian**'s fiery energy will fan the flames of arousal. Hold a palm stone or wand between your palms while you are waiting for your lover to arrive in bed. Close your eyes. Breathe deeply and slowly. Meditate, and let your fantasies fill your mind as the red carnelian's energy permeates the bedroom. Imagine your deepest, most secret sexual desires. Feel the fervor flow into the stone, and back through your body. After a few minutes, put the stone down and watch the sparks fly.

Another stone to keep by the bedside is **red jasper**, which rejuvenates sexual urges, creating an aura of sexual energy in the bedroom that will arouse both mind and body. In short, it gets the blood pumping to the right organs. Red jasper is great for men who are struggling with erectile dysfunction or women who want a boost to their libido, and its fun, creative power will prolong a sexual experience. Slip this crystal under your mattress before you get busy for a long night of fun.

Leanne's favorite stone is garnet, which she wears in jewelry and tucks into her mattress. It has helped enhance her confidence both in and out of the bedroom with its regenerative energy. Garnet is a passionate stone that brings out both sensuality and sexuality, turning her into a femme fatale. Try it for yourself: Wear a garnet pendant or ring the next time you want to feel like a hottie, and watch how others react.

SEXPOT RED HOT TEA

Drop a clean, tumbled or faceted **garnet** into a pot of boiling water for three minutes, and then use it to pour yourself a cup of tea with cinnamon. Sandra highly recommends Stash Spice Dragon Red Chai in particular, which contains cinnamon, ginger root, and cloves, all of which are associated with love and sex magic, and it is made with rooibos, which is naturally decaffeinated. Or you can make your own version with a combination of these spices. Sip this tea to pre-game for a wild night.

COME ROCK MY WORLD CHARM BAG

Place a teaspoon of cinnamon chips with a garnet stone (tumbled or faceted) into a red charm bag. Anoint it with rose oil, and hang it above your bed or tuck it into your pillowcase to project an aura of fiery passion to attract the object(s) of your desire.

THIS NEXT SEXERCISE IS RATED X FOR "XTRA FUN" . . .

There is vast power in the energy that is created by lovers prior to climax. The intensity of the force that is generated can provide a serious zap to your magic that you can unlock whenever you need it—if you capture it properly. Here's one of Sandra's favorite ways to make the most of it: Find a matching pair of quartz crystal points and place one in each of your hands, then grasp hands with your lover, pressing the crystals between your palms while you are having intercourse or pleasuring each other, as long as it doesn't require you to use your hands. As soon as one of you is nearing orgasm, let go of the crystals as close to the release as possible. After, you can each carry one of the crystals and tap into the juice of that ecstasy (see what we did there?) to achieve your goals by using it as a battery to boost the voltage of any spell. Place it in the center of a crystal grid, carry it alongside other stones in any charm bag, or wear it in a crystal cage as a pendant when you want to feel connected through your shared passion. Recharge the crystals in the same way only when you feel your desire is strong and your energy level is high.

7

SELF-CARE AND RELAXATION: CRYSTALS IN THE BATH

The bathroom is a place of true privacy, although parents (of humans or pets!) may disagree. The bathroom's focus is truly on the self. It is typically the first place that people face their own image each day. Perhaps more than any other room in the home, this is where we are focused on our own daily personal maintenance, and the realities of some of our most basic physical needs. Crystals and stones can support our efforts to refresh ourselves and prepare us to embrace whatever we encounter as we begin each day, as well as wash away any stress or negativity we have picked up from the day's events.

Natural minerals have been used for decades to outfit bathrooms, from countertops and sinks to elaborate tubs and showers. While we have both dreamed of a bathroom overhaul that would include a giant amethyst bathtub or a rose quartz sink, you don't need to remodel an entire room to bring big crystal energy into your self-care castle. There are much easier, less expensive ways to incorporate water-safe stones into your space to blend in with your décor and become an integral part of your daily self-care rituals.

SHOWER POWER

Combining crystals and meditation in the bath is a healthy practice that anyone can incorporate into their daily routines and is especially easy for beginners. It starts with taking a more conscious approach to breathing. Air is the literal breath of life, and taking a few moments at any time of day to focus on breathing with purpose is beneficial to body, mind, and spirit. Controlled breathing has been proven to have medical benefits, like lowering blood pressure and releasing stress, which builds up and wreaks havoc on our well-being.

COME ON IN, THE WATER'S FINE:
WHICH CRYSTALS ARE BATHROOM-SAFE

Any crystals you place as part of the décor should be polished stones that you are sure will be safe in the humidity associated with the bathroom. Choose crystals that will not break down or dissolve due to the damp environment: The stones should not be absorbent, brittle, soft, or untreated. The Mohs hardness scale is one criterion for water safety, but it is not the only one, especially since many stones fall within a range on that scale. (See https://geology.com/minerals/mohs-hardness-scale.shtml for a list of common minerals and their ratings. Those rated 5 or below should not be used in water.)

We have personally used the following stones safely in our own bathrooms:

Many types of agate
Clear, rose, or smoky quartz
Amethyst
Shungite
Yellow or blue calcite
Bloodstone
White, red, or black moonstone
Aventurine
Carnelian
Citrine
Tiger's eye
Howlite

Sandra works with a handful of crystals in the morning, and a different set at night, and each of them is chosen for specific intentions. You can create your own simple meditation by choosing a few crystals to work with that represent the traits you wish to exhibit, or the things you hope to achieve, in the short or long term. You may choose to focus on specific powers of the stones at different times; when you arise and enter the shower, you might hold an amethyst to strengthen your resolve to cease a bad habit. Before bed, you might hold that same amethyst as you take a relaxing bath to tune in to your intuition in the hopes of gaining psychic wisdom in your dreams that night. Try focusing on a single goal for each session at first, and when you see good results, you can add others.

CLARIFYING CRYSTAL BREATHWORK

This can be done while sitting in the tub or on the edge of the tub after a shower.

- Hold your chosen crystal in your nondominant hand. You can choose a crystal that is associated with your purpose, or you can use a cleansed clear quartz.

- Think about what you hope that stone will help you accomplish, and take a slow breath in through your nose for a count of four, hold it for a count of four, and then push the breath out through your pursed lips for a count of four.

- If you need to decide between two courses of action, do this twice; think of each choice in turn, and then note how your body feels toward each.

- If you are hoping to create something, do this three times, opening yourself up to inspiration.

- If you want to solidify something, do this four times, feeling the sense of stability.

RUB-A-DUB-DUB,
WORK YOUR MAGIC IN THE TUB!

There are a number of bath products that include crystals and stones. The same way that we use soap to dissolve the physical dirt and other unwanted substances that cling to our skin, we can incorporate crystals to release emotional, spiritual, and mundane impurities and clear up energy blocks, allowing us to operate at our best.

Leanne uses a soap that is infused with aventurine, citrine, sage, and sea salt to project for luck and success. Aventurine is linked with building careers and accomplishments. It is celebrated for giving its owners opportunity and luck. Aventurine is known to entice luck and prosperity. The stone gets its name from the Italian word *aventura*, which means "by chance." Leanne carries aventurine with her in a gold charm bag when she travels to Las Vegas, and keeps one in her makeup bag to feel beautiful and showered with abundance, no pun intended! The citrine adds inspiration and the spirit of fresh ideas and growth. The sea salt is great for cleaning negativity off the body and allows calm to enter the mind. Sage is wonderful for banishing all residual pessimism. As she washes, Leanne visualizes all the mundane thoughts and clutter melting off her body and soul, clearing the way for the blessings she envisions.

EASY SPELL BATH RECIPES

Combine these crystals and other ingredients from your cupboard into a muslin pouch, and add to your running bathwater to soak in their magic!

- Shungite and calendula petals to fortify and repair the skin, and remove negativity

- Rose quartz and elderflower to relieve inflammation and to amplify loving vibes

- Carnelian and peppermint to wipe the slate clean, and invoke main-character energy only!

- Smoky quartz with sea salt to feel safe and grounded, especially after a challenging situation

Morning Mirror Meditation

Despite the fact that Leanne has built a successful career as a psychic and medium, she still occasionally suffers from imposter syndrome. Like many people, she has mornings when she wants to crawl back into the safe comfort of her bed. On difficult days, rather than hiding and staying home, she begins her morning mirror meditation with a tiger's eye in her hand, boosting her confidence, grounding her in her purpose, and protecting her from negative self-talk. While standing facing the bathroom mirror, she then holds a blue calcite to squelch anxiety and mood swings, followed by a green aventurine to protect her spirit from psychic vampires—people who relentlessly demand her time and attention for their own personal gains, depleting her energy.

Self-Defense Is Self-Care

One common morning ritual for both of us and many other Witches we know is protection, and we have wards that help keep us safe from harm in the physical as well as the spiritual sense. Some of our favorite crystals that we use as we prepare to venture out each day are **black tourmaline**, **obsidian**, and **jet**. These stones help us bolster our psychic boundaries, so we connect with them as part of our "getting ready to go" routines. On days that we don't have time for an elaborate ritual, simply touching these stones and repeating a mantra, such as "I am fully and completely protected from all harm," before heading out the door recharges our shields.

BETTER THAN COFFEE: WAKING UP WITH CARNELIAN

Maybe you're not a morning person, or you're having one of those mornings when you feel like you ran a marathon in your sleep. **Carnelian** will give you a much-needed zap of vigor without the caffeine aftereffects. Place a carnelian in your bath or on the edge of your shower for a boost. Need a kick in the butt to get you moving? Carnelian will reboot your motivation. It is a wonderful stone for people who need help in creativity and recall.

Carnelian can also alleviate "I'm too tired" syndrome. It promotes sexuality and passion, so it's just as welcome in the getting-ready-for-bed rinse-off. Commonly used to elevate moods and relieve depression, it can help create the right mind-set for intimacy.

THE BENEFITS OF SKIN-CARE RITUALS ARE CRYSTAL CLEAR

In recent years, crystal-based beauty tools have become extremely popular; they are available everywhere from department and beauty supply stores to big-box outlets. The positive effects from incorporating crystals and stones in skin care are well documented. Combined with centuries-old methods, these crystal implements can increase circulation, allowing toxins to be released. Increased oxygen flow decreases lines and puffiness and revives tired skin. For best results, use these tools with oils and moisturizers to help with nutrient absorption, and remember to wash them after each use. Here are some suggestions from our own beauty toolboxes:

ROSE QUARTZ EYE CONTOUR MASSAGE TOOLS

The link between rose quartz and beauty goes all the way back to the ancient Egyptians, who believed that rose quartz granted youth and had anti-aging properties: It is said that the goddess Isis would gather rose quartz crystals by the Nile River to keep Her complexion perfect. Rose quartz is the MVP when it comes to all kinds of love, but it also eases tension and quiets anger with its gentle, soothing vibes. It puts you in touch with your emotions, particularly one of the most important of all: compassion. So often we find it easier to have compassion for others rather than for ourselves. This soft-pink crystal has been used for centuries to heal both the emotional and physical body, as well as the link between them, and can be used effectively to combat negative body image. Rose quartz reminds us that we are deserving of love, especially from ourselves. These contour tools are carved into a shape reminiscent of a mushroom, making them easy to hold and maneuver carefully over the eye area. They can be kept in the refrigerator to deliver a deeper cooling sensation on a hot day. First, apply a moisturizer to your skin (without getting any in your eyes). **While gently guiding the rose quartz tool over your eye area, open yourself to the loving, peaceful energy as it sinks into your skin. Look upon your own reflection with softer eyes, and see your true inner and outer beauty taking shape as you release negative thought patterns.**

AMETHYST FACE ROLLERS

Probably the most common of these tools, the amethyst face roller is the stress buster you need after a long day. For those struggling with sleep issues, amethyst is perfect for an evening bathroom ritual. This tension-releasing technique combined with the powers of the stone will relax your face muscles, tame your anxiety, and help bring balance to your hormones and your nervous system. Using the roller will boost collagen production and promote healing to blemishes. The tranquillity amethyst provides to mind and body will show on your face the next morning, as you wake up less puffy, more rested, and mentally serene.

Follow these easy steps:

1. Apply a moisturizer, facial oil, or serum to prepare the skin.

2. Work from the center of your face to the sides, gently pushing the tool upward and outward. Lift up when you reach the edge of your face and return to the starting point; do not drag the tool back and forth across the skin. The idea is to move in one direction only.

3. Massage each section three to five times before moving to the next section: chin toward ears, cheeks toward ears, under eyes toward ears, brows toward hairline. Then starting at the hairline, roll down the sides of the face toward the neck.

JADE GUA SHA MASSAGE TOOLS

Arguably the most advanced of the three tools we're discussing, the gua sha is the primary tool of an ancient Chinese healing technique known as gua sha, designed to move the chi energy (life-force) responsible for inflammation, promoting lymphatic drainage. Regular practice has a profound effect on wrinkles, age spots, puffiness, and other symptoms; some people find that this treatment even helps them drain their sinuses!

Gua sha is not limited to the face; it is performed on many other areas of the body to reduce inflammation. It has also been known to help with migraines, chronic neck pain, menopausal symptoms, and

Please note: We value the origins of this wisdom and highly recommend learning the proper gua sha technique from a Chinese medical skin-care professional. You can find beginner tutorials on YouTube. *(If you have a skin condition or blood pressure or heart issues, discuss your desire to use this tool with your doctor before beginning your regimen.)* Our personal choice is Sandra Lanshin Chiu, LAc, an acupuncturist and herbalist who specializes in treating and rejuvenating skin through the practice of Traditional Chinese Medicine.

other ailments. The gentle version of it is perfect for contouring the face and neck area. This tool is used with facial oil so that it glides over the skin, just like the other tools discussed.

The most appropriate stone for a gua sha massage tool is jade, given its history. Long revered for its physical and metaphysical qualities alike, jade has been carved into all manner of objects, both sacred and mundane, for centuries. It is believed that jade's energies help to balance emotions and bring peace. Jade is a gentle protective stone that is a natural defense against jealousy and envy. Long prized as a lucky charm, it is believed to improve the powers of intuition, promoting tranquillity and harmony. Perhaps its most appropriate attribute when it comes to beauty is its reputation for bestowing a form of immortality upon its owner.

Ultimately, the incorporation of all these crystals puts us in touch with the healing powers of the earth in a tangible, direct way every day, as we add the elements of water to cleanse us, air to refresh and balance us, and the fire of our own desires to propel us forward toward our greater happiness.

8

PARTNERSHIP AND PRODUCTIVITY: CRYSTALS IN THE WORKPLACE

Even great jobs present challenges when it comes to navigating personal politics and normal workplace stressors, including looming deadlines, people you're not a fan of, client complaints, and interactions that leave you with frayed nerves and low morale. Stones and crystals can foster stronger partnerships in the office and keep you calm, cool, and collected, even on a bad day. They will be your daily cheerleaders, motivating and inspiring you, and putting some wind right back in your sails.

EMPOWER YOURSELF, YOUR STAFF, AND EVEN YOUR BOSS

Crystals are not only functional, they are also beautiful—and surrounding yourself with beauty is always a sensational idea, no matter where you are. Incorporating them into your workspace can take off some of that harsh fluorescent-light edge. Whether you own a business or are just jazzing up your office, attractive stones will fuel the soul while you get your job done, especially if you pair them with indoor-loving plants, like pothos. Just remember to use your best judgment; it's easy to go from a pleasant ambience to an office distraction if you're not careful. It's also important to safeguard crystals (and other treasures) if your office isn't secure after hours.

Speaking of distractions, background interferences like social media and office gossip cost companies money and prevent employee growth. A strategically placed tower or sphere of **fluorite** will help you focus and concentrate better than a cup of coffee. Fluorite removes mental blocks and minimizes disruptions, and has been a workplace go-to for both of us for years. We both wear fluorite bracelets to remedy brain fog, broken concentration, and writer's block. In fact, our fluorite jewelry powered this book as well as our two previous ones. It's a must-have for any creative.

If you're feeling overwhelmed by a project and need to push through, **bloodstone** will increase your endurance, determination, and

FIVE CRYSTALS TO ENRICH YOUR WORKSPACES

Citrine—manifests success, building wealth

Carnelian—promotes leadership, supports motivation, and builds morale

Smoky quartz—keeps the negativity at bay, protects positive vibes

Black tourmaline—reduces brain fog and stress, stabilizes a hectic or chaotic period

Lodestone—attracts sales, clients, and business opportunities. Be sure to "feed" it by covering it with iron filings, which you can generally find at metaphysical shops, in person or online. Feeding your lodestone increases its effectiveness as well as your own by focusing your intent.

courage; adjust your response to stressful situations; and boost your natural talents and abilities. You can place it in your environment, but it's even more effective when worn as jewelry or carried in your pocket as you move through your day.

We all know that the pressure does not end when the business day does. Work stress often follows us home, affecting our family life and health. Difficulties in the workplace can lead to complications such as insomnia, depression, addictive behaviors, and physical illness, which can lead to a vicious cycle of sick days and reduced work performance. Try this easy meditation practice for just a few minutes at the start and end of a shift to make a big difference in your ability to tune out the noise when you're off duty.

Opening Procedures:
Quick Crystal Meditation to Begin the Workday

- Sit in your office chair, or if your job doesn't have one, find a quiet place to sit at your work. (Yes, a bathroom stall counts!)

- Hold a crystal—or more—that contains the energy you want to bring into yourself in your nondominant hand, and a crystal that contains the energy you want to project into your environment in your dominant hand. If you are ambidextrous, choose which way the energy will flow through you, in one hand and out the other. Alternatively, crystals can be placed on your right or your left side, and you can focus the energy moving through you that way.

- As you inhale, think of a word that describes what you want to bring into yourself. We have used words like *positivity*, *inspiration*, *success*, and *joy*. As you take slow, deep, purposeful breaths, you may repeat the same word(s) more than once for emphasis, like a mantra.

FIVE OF NATURE'S BEST
WORK-STRESS RELIEVERS

Amethyst—relieves mental pressure and restores cool, calm, and collected vibes, even on the worst day

Amazonite—this ultimate chill pill soothes frayed nerves

Blue calcite—maintains the balance between the heart and the mind

Blue lace agate—promotes empathy and careful communication when tempers rise

Sodalite—the "stone of peace" supports cooperation and teamwork

---

- As you exhale, think of a word that describes what you want to project into the workplace for each breath. Some we like: *leadership, productivity, camaraderie,* and *mastery.*

- This should take around five minutes, but you can spend as much time as you need to feel ready for the day . . . just don't be late for your shift!

GET THAT MIDAS TOUCH (SECURE THE BAG)

Get noticed and attract customers by placing **green aventurine** and **pyrite** around your business cards; if you set them out on a table, place the stones with them. If you keep them in a holder in a computer bag, briefcase, or shoulder bag, tuck the stones in with them. The rewards that aventurine and pyrite bring to a person's professional life run the gamut from attracting money to keeping emotions in check. Specifically, aventurine encourages new opportunities and optimism, while pyrite amplifies prosperity and growth. The pair work together to elevate your energy and bolster confidence, particularly when you encounter rejection, as every entrepreneur does from time to time.

Meanwhile, a tumbled **citrine**, known as the "the merchant's stone," belongs in the safe or cash drawer of every retail business. Its golden hue shines like the sun to burn away economic slumps and stimulate growth, welcoming in abundance and prosperity. Just seeing it reminds us of the wise old saying "You catch more flies with honey than vinegar," which anyone in customer service would do well to note.

BEATING THE INEVITABLE "BAD DAYS"

Everyone has a bad day now and then (some more than others). Half the work at any job can be dealing with your colleagues. Since it is counterproductive to throw rocks at disagreeable customers or co-workers, we suggest hugging a crystal instead. Tightly. (Wink!) In all seriousness, though, your work environment matters to your mental and financial stability, and the stress you accumulate from dealing with any hostility there takes a toll.

Carry **black obsidian** to shield and protect from emotional attacks on your work ethic and personality. You could even place a small obsidian mirror on your desk to deflect the b.s. A **black tourmaline** tower absorbs the negativity from any space, transforming jealousy and competitiveness into motivation and cooperation. It's also gorgeous (and less conspicuous) worn in jewelry—and safer than dueling swords. There are days when people get so wrapped up in their emotions and day-to-day lives that teamwork can be a real challenge. When the squad seems scattered, the peaceful vibration of **amethyst** is a lifesaver. Place an amethyst cluster on the table at the next company meeting or Zoom call to bring harmony and a sense of community.

A Final Word on the Workplace Drama

We spend many of our waking hours at work, so the environment there inevitably will affect your life both in and out of the office. But if a workplace is so noxious that it is affecting your sleep, mental state, and home life, all the gemstones in the earth may not help. If your gut is telling you it is a lost cause, it's time to polish up that résumé, grab your crystals, and get out.

Our Crystal Recommendations for Various Professions

All of the stones we discuss in this chapter can bring countless benefits to anyone, but we've also developed effective prescriptions tailored for specific lines of work—Earth's tried-and-true "vitamins and minerals" to support the dedicated, industrious, and often overwhelmed workforce.

Frontline Medical Workers— Doctors, Nurses, and EMTs

We put our trust—and our very lives—in the hands of emergency medical technicians, nurses, and doctors every day. Those on the front lines of the battle against disease need protection and healing, too. It is imperative for them to recharge and guard their energy. Bringing crystals and stones into a place where care is given and received can raise its vibrations, support heroic efforts, and improve the dynamics between patients and their caregivers.

No matter your field, in order to mend others, you must first safeguard yourself, and one of the best crystals for reinvigorating any medical professional is **prehnite**. This soft-green, almost glowing stone is said to "heal the healer," even in the most demanding situations. When worn or activated and placed in an emergency setting, it alleviates trauma to both the body and soul.

To settle the anxiety of a waiting room, ambulance, or dental office, nothing soothes like **amazonite**. This Xanax of the crystal world calms anxiety and fear, but it also improves communication when searching for the root of the problem. Leanne has a dental hygienist client who taped amazonite and **rose quartz** to the dreaded chair to promote a sense of peace in her patients. Tumbled stones, palm stones, and wands will mollify nervous hands. Or pick a beautiful pendant that lands the stone on your chest just above your heart and it will relax your pounding pulse.

THE FUTURE OF THE WORLD—
TEACHERS AND DAY CARE WORKERS

We have the utmost respect for the teachers who mold our future generations. Children and teens have boundless energy, and it can be a challenge, to say the least, to hold their attention. Sandra's mother taught various grades, from first grade to high school, and Sandra actually went to college to be a secondary school teacher before life led her into teaching in a whole other way. Here are our suggestions for these underappreciated superheroes.

Rich, vibrant blue-and-green **chrysocolla**, reminiscent of the way our planet looks from outer space, brings out the ability of educators to transform lives through the sharing of wisdom, and reminds us all that the way we treat children and others in front of them has a direct impact on the climate of our society. **Blue calcite** releases communication blocks, allowing students to open up to more positive interaction in the classroom and focus their attention on the lesson at hand. It can also help teachers to find the right words to pass on their knowledge in an effective way.

For students with attention issues, we especially recommend **fluorite** and **hematite**, which support our efforts to stay grounded and centered. Fluorite enhances organizational skills, to keep projects and assignments on track. Spending a few minutes experiencing the dense heaviness and cool smoothness of a hematite palm stone will restore balance and alignment, like a mineral weighted blanket for your mind. Sandra has one for home and one for work, and they have been regular parts of her practice for decades.

To incorporate crystals into your classroom in a creative way, keep a bowl of assorted tumbled stones in your desk. Choose a different student each day to pick one out to discuss as a class. Before telling them the traditional lore of the crystal, let them feel it and guess what it might be known for. You'll be surprised at how often they get it right.

Balancing the Scales of Justice— Officers of the Law, Lawyers, and Judges

When the world brings us turmoil, it is crucial to keep safe the people who protect and serve us. Most of us cannot imagine the trauma, stress, and fear that officers of the law encounter on the job. People who uphold the scales of justice spend years training and preparing themselves for this intense work, and each decision they make can save or destroy lives. Unfortunately, too many of the folks who are responsible for our society's well-being suffer from post-traumatic stress and other emotional strain that can compromise their judgment. If that sounds familiar, these are the stones we recommend reaching for:

Red jasper magnifies truth and integrity in any situation. It is a power stone for anyone whose job is to rectify wrongdoing. Traditionally associated with the planet Mars, which is named for the god of war, it is believed to supply miraculous strength to those who stand against injustice. To balance its fiery energy, carry a **blue lace agate** alongside, whose humble, soothing vibration encourages us to remain level-headed and walk the path of honor and humanity, no matter what chaos surrounds us.

When the day ends and it is time to decompress, sleep with a tumbled **clear quartz** and a **black tourmaline** under your pillow. This combination will bring peace and allow for restorative rest by clearing residual stress and apprehension, repairing emotional damage, and supporting a feeling of safety and security.

Show Me the Money—
Bankers, Accountants, and Investment Advisors

Money might make the world go 'round, but it is the people who push the papers and crunch the numbers that make those stacks of cash grow. Recently, crystals that can attract prosperity and make wise investments have become a prized asset to many financial professionals we know. In particular, stockbrokers and investment advisors will benefit from keeping **malachite** and **pyrite** in any space where they speak with clients. That combination puts people in the mind-set to take the necessary steps that bring prosperity. And whenever the market takes an inevitable downward turn, whether big or small, taking a quick meditation break with a **smoky quartz** will clear negative thoughts and fears and get you back in a growth mentality.

The Heartbeat of Business—
Administrative Assistants, Store Managers, and
Sales and Customer Service Representatives

The unsung heroes of any business are the people with boots on the ground, the ones who do the daily jobs that keep a company running and are the stabilizing glue that holds a workplace together. They deal directly with customers and are often the face of the business. Leanne is a proud graduate of Katharine Gibbs School, where she received an associate degree in Secretarial Sciences. Even though the word *secre-*

tary has fallen out of fashion, the responsibility of any executive assistant or customer service representative is the same: serving the public as well as the higher-ups.

Your daily to-do list can get overwhelming, especially when there are always fires that need to be put out. Balancing your priorities is difficult when everything appears to be crucial. When emergencies are at the front of mind, it can seem counterproductive to take a moment to connect with your crystals; but trust us, it pays off in the long run.

Keep these tumbled stones where you can get at them: **smoky quartz, pink zebra jasper,** and **lapis lazuli**. This combination will help you rise above the chaos, think clearly, respond rather than react, and keep your chin up when the turkeys are determined to get you down. You can also add a **red tiger's eye** for extra strength and resilience. Whenever the stress sets in, step away from your desk for a few minutes and hold these crystals in your hands. Do a simple breathing exercise to get yourself back to level: inhale for a count of five, hold for a count of five, exhale for a count of five, and hold for a count of five before inhaling again. Do this at least three times while feeling the stones in your hands, and you'll be good to go.

CREATIVE GENIUS—
MUSICIANS, ARTISTS, WRITERS, AND ACTORS

The creatives among us have the power to influence and transform the world. Music evolves and heals the soul. Art reflects and refracts

THREE MUSES CHARM BAG

The three muses of Greek lore were said to possess the power to make people forget their pain and struggles. This is why so many people seek out entertainment in its many forms: It can give us a much-needed break from our daily battles.

- The bag should reflect the personality of the artist: Perhaps it is a well-worn leather pouch, a hand-me-down kiss lock coin purse from the 1970s, or a classic vintage purple-and-gold Crown Royal bag.

- Add three tumbled stones that bring the power, passion, and pleasure: **carnelian**, **citrine**, and **malachite**. Citrine clears creative blocks. (You may substitute **pyrite** for citrine if you are particularly hoping to earn a living doing your art.) Carnelian will bring brave new ideas, stimulating any creative soul. Malachite will manifest the vision with abundant rewards upon completion.

- Add something that symbolizes your artform: a guitar pick (you can find these made from your own birthstone), a small charm in the shape of a palette, a lens cap . . . you're the creative. Come up with an item that means something to you.

- Place the items into the bag, and carry it with you to a place that you would like to showcase your art. Hold it against your heart, and say, aloud or in your mind,

> *"I invoke the Muses Three.*
> *Inspiration, come to me;*
> *Transformation, flow through me.*
> *Turn pain to joy! So shall it be."*
>
> · Anoint the charm bag with a solar oil, like orange or lemon, and keep it with you when you are doing your thing. Rock on.

our lives and opens the mind to fresh possibilities. Writing makes us receptive to exploration and new ideas. Tattoos use the body as a canvas, allowing self-expression to take on a physical form. When creative people bless us with their talents, they are nurtured in turn by the reverberation of their art and how it matters. Crystals can also support, motivate, and energize them when they need an extra boost, or just everyday inspiration.

When Sandra rode along with her mom running errands, her mother would teach her the songs she sang with her first graders, and she's been singing them ever since. Rock 'n' roll is the soundtrack of her soul, but she loves all kinds of music. When performing with her band, she has always chosen her stage jewelry to reflect her mood and her intentions for each performance. Often, she reaches for **Herkimer diamonds** because they amplify energy so well, and live music is all about the energetic exchange between the band and the audience.

Wearing them, particularly as pendants, sends the vibration right from the heart, through the vocal chords, and outward to entertain and enchant everyone within earshot. She has been known to keep her go-to creative charm bag in her gig bag with her microphone (and her signature "white wing dove" shawl).

9

SACRED SPACE:
CRYSTALS IN THE TEMPLE

If you consider yourself a spiritual person, you may have a room, or a corner of one, dedicated to your practice. Even if you don't—but especially if you're thinking about it—consider adding crystals to your spiritual practice, and your space.

Why dedicate a temple in your home? It's powerful to have a des-ignated place to connect with your higher power, regardless of what religion or path you're on. Even if you belong to a religion that has public places of worship, and even if you believe (as many of us do) that God is everywhere, you may still wish to create your own sacred space.

Your home temple or shrine should be located as far away from high-traffic areas as is practical and kept separate from most of your mundane daily activities. It needs to feel special in order to provoke an aura of sanctity. Some of our daily routines don't necessarily disturb the ambience of blessedness, such as acts of self-care or caring for oth-ers in that same space. (This is why the bedroom is a common choice as host for hallowing.)

There are countless ways to bring crystals into your temple setting, but four in particular that we regularly practice: meditation, devotion, divination, and spirit communication.

MEDITATION

Over the years, we've had many clients tell us they "can't meditate." Usually, this is because they have preconceived notions about what meditation *is*, like that your mind has to be completely blank. This sets the bar impossibly high for beginners. On the contrary, a good place to start is what may be referred to as **insight meditation**. In this method, you sit comfortably, close your eyes, relax, and rather than trying to "blank your mind," you take in everything around you, beginning with your own breath rising and falling. You don't even have to breathe especially deeply. Allow your breath to naturally occur, and center your attention on the rising and falling of your midsection. With insight meditation, you just continue to allow all sensations to come and go as you passively note each one. To connect with and benefit from your crystals, choose the stones that are most likely to help you meet your meditation goal, and hold them in the appropriate hand or place them on the appropriate side of your body, depending on what you would like to achieve. For instance, if you would like to begin each day drawing in peace and positivity and projecting confidence and capability, you may choose to hold a **carnelian** in your dominant hand and a **lepidolite** in the other.

Another form we practice often is **visualization meditation**: the use of mental images to influence bodily processes (like healing), control pain, prepare for a performance, or achieve a particular goal. We hold specific crystals as we picture our desired outcome, or visualize positive images to ground and center us.

When you are ready to try a more advanced form of meditation—and it's up to you what constitutes "ready"—you can explore **concentration meditation**. Sit comfortably and pay exclusive attention to one thing, which could be a physical object like a crystal pyramid, or a spoken mantra, which is a word or phrase that expresses a goal or intent. It is typical for the mind to stray; the goal is to pull your attention back to the focus each time without judgment or concern. This process teaches us how to stay grounded as we move through the challenges of our daily lives. Stones like **smoky quartz, black tourmaline,** and **hematite** are excellent choices for grounding, but this technique can also be used to manifest goals, so the focus crystal could be any that supports your ambitions.

Devotion

Crystals have played a role in the adoration of the gods since ancient times (remember the breastplate of the high priest from chapter 1?), as both are associated with certain powers. The modern popularity of both has given us plenty of choices when it comes to altar décor. Look for beautiful statues of deities—some are even carved out of crystals—large altar stones, ritual tools like wands and bowls, candle holders (**selenite** is Sandra's favorite for an altar), and carvings of animal totems and other symbols for use in the rites and rituals in your temple.

When you are forming a relationship with a particular deity, one of the best ways to strengthen it is to make **crystal offerings**. (Some offerings may be left outside the home, but we are focusing on the temple in your house for now.) Gifting a special stone to gods, saints, or angels will open communication and form a bond with these powerful energies. The gods and spirits may not need or require our offerings, but a pretty crystal or gem will certainly attract Their attention and invite the Divine into our lives. When we make offerings, we are showing gratitude and love to higher power.

Think about what your chosen deity is said to represent or govern, and choose stones that are associated with Them. If you want to reach out to a goddess who is affiliated with a particular planet, for example, leave stones ruled by that planet at the base of a statue or against the frame of an image on your altar or shrine with a few spoken words to declare your intent (and if you don't have a statue or artwork, the crystal is still an attractive offering on its own). Sandra's statues of Hygeia and Apollo stand amid a bed of healing crystals, and her statue of Hera has peacock ore, titanium aura crystals, and sparkling pyrites at her feet. The moonstone that Leanne placed at the base of her statue of the Moon Goddess Diana forms an astral bridge between them. Like the goddess, moonstone boosts inspiration, supports intuition, and provides maternal protection.

We recommend wearing these crystals to stay connected to divinity all day:

Blessed Mother Mary	Rose quartz, Apophyllite, and Kunzite
Apollo, Helios, and Lugh	Sunstone, Amber, and Sapphire
Artemis, Diana, and Selene	Moonstone and Selenite
Archangel Michael	Sugilite
Archangel Gabriel	Citrine
Archangel Raphael	Malachite
Archangel Uriel	Amber

Divination

Best for Beginners: The Crystal Pendulum

Pendulums are some of the oldest tools for divination; their use is believed to predate written history. The pendulum is basically a pointed object placed on a string or chain. The object can be made of wood, metal, or other materials, but our favorites are made of crystals. They are used to answer simple yes-or-no questions, but they have also been used as dowsing tools. Some healers suspend them over the bodies of their patients to locate medical issues, and certain psychics dangle them over wares in the market to choose their talismans. Others have held them over maps to find treasures or locate missing persons. They figure prominently in Italian folk magic: grandmothers swear they can discover the gender of babies by dangling a common pin at the end of a thread. Ultimately, no matter what they are used for, the psychic power comes from the person holding the pendulum . . . but the crystal helps connect that person to spirit, or their own higher self, to provide the clarity and direction.

CONNECTING TO YOUR PENDULUM

Once you have chosen your pendulum (or, more likely, it has chosen you), the next step is to form a bond with it. Like a friend, connect with the crystal by keeping it close. The more you work with it, the better it will work for you. If it is a water-safe crystal, start by cleaning and clearing it with water and letting it dry in the sun; if you have any doubts, clean it with a soft cloth and cleanse its energy with the smoke of frankincense and myrrh or a similar incense from your practice. You may anoint it with a drop of lavender oil, or a blended oil that is formulated for psychic power and divination. Then, hold it in the palm of your dominant hand, or place it on a charging plate, and imbue it with your energy and intention. You may speak some words aloud, such as:

"I bring to life
This pendulum of stone;
May every truth
To my mind now be known."

WORKING WITH THE PENDULUM

When first working with a pendulum, hold the end in the hand that feels natural, grasping the end of the chain or string between your thumb and your index finger.

Begin by finding out how your specific pendulum indicates yes and no.

First, ask it a question for which you know the answer is yes. For instance, "Is my legal name _____?" and speak your legal name. When it moves in a specific direction repeatedly, you know that movement is a yes. This is commonly a vertical swing, like nodding up and down, but it doesn't have to be.

Next, ask it a question that's a definite no, like, "Am I asleep?" Watch how it moves again. It should swing in a different way. The most likely direction is horizontal, like shaking your own head no, but again, it doesn't have to be.

Then, ask it to show you what "maybe" looks like. Often, this will be a circular motion, as if it cannot decide.

Once you have established these motions, ask questions you don't know the answer to, and note the movements. We always recommend keeping a written record of your divinations in a safe, private journal to refer back to later.

THE CLASSIC DIVINATORY TOOL: THE CRYSTAL BALL

The iconic image of a fortune teller sitting in front of a glowing sphere is the first thing that comes to people's minds when they hear the words *crystal ball*. Crystal balls are much more than carnival parlor tricks, however. They act as windows to the clairvoyant mind by harnessing psychic energy to provide information about the future, the present, and the past. The use of crystal balls for divination can be traced back to the ancient druids, who polished balls of beryl to offer wisdom and deliver messages and guidance. In the Victorian era, crystal balls saw a surge in popularity, and practitioners claimed it was best to use the ball "when the sun was at its northernmost declination." Through a cloud in the glass, an image would appear.

Peering into the future may be their best-known use, but crystal balls have many applications and come in a variety of materials. Those who work with healing the body often also work with crystal balls to harness energy to transfer to those who are in pain or ill. They may be 100 percent **clear quartz crystal**, or they may be made from clarified quartz, reconstituted quartz crystal, or glass. When choosing a crystal ball, pick one that connects with you. If you can, take time to hold it before you purchase it. Not everyone will resonate with a clear crystal to work with for scrying. Depending on the type of psychic work you plan to do with it, you'll need to harness specific energy. Leanne has two crystal balls: one is made of **lapis lazuli** to speak with the dead, and the other of **rose quartz** to invigorate her love readings. As with all crystal work, find a ball that speaks to you.

PREPARING TO SCRY WITH YOUR CRYSTAL BALL

Once you choose a crystal ball, it is time to take it home and prepare it for magical use. Depending on the material it's made of, you can wash it with mild soap and water. A good wash banishes not just unwanted energy but fingerprints as well, for a clearer reading. Next, pass the ball over frankincense, sage, or a similar cleansing smoke to remove negative vibrations. The night before you use the ball for the first time (and whenever you give it a good cleansing), place it in a safe place where it can absorb moonlight—ideally on the night of a full moon.

If you haven't created a temple room or sacred space, this would be an ideal time to designate one. It should be comfortable and quiet, and it doesn't have to be large; it could be a corner of your bedroom or a walk-in closet. Wherever you choose, cleanse and bless the area with incense, such as frankincense and myrrh, nag champa, or something similar. Sit in a comfortable position, holding the sphere in your hands, and introduce yourself to your ball. You may choose to recite the following spell that Leanne has used with great success over the years:

"Ball of crystal, ball of light,
Grant me now the gift of sight."

CONDUCTING THE READING

When you are ready to begin your reading, place the crystal ball on a dark cloth or crystal ball stand directly in front of you. Lighting two white candles on each side will help illuminate images in your mind. Note that we all experience messages in our own ways. Some psychics say images appear like a movie. Others say the missives form like thoughts in their mind, the information flowing directly into their consciousness. In any case, the crystal ball is a tool to unlock your psychic abilities, so your mind-set is as critical as the setting. Banish doubt from your mind, relax, and open yourself up to receive psychic information.

The first time you work with the crystal ball, set aside between 15 and 30 minutes. Give yourself enough time to settle into a steady pattern of breathing (you could try insight meditation to get into the right headspace), and then follow these steps:

- Close your eyes and take three deep breaths.

- Open your eyes and look into the ball.

- Soften your gaze; the ball should begin to appear fuzzy, cloudy, or hazy.

- Allow thoughts to take shape in your mind without judgment.

- When you feel you are done, give gratitude to the tool that gave you this knowledge.

- For best results, record the thoughts, images, smells, and any other sensations in a journal so you can refer back to them later. This will help you develop your practice.

Anyone can scry with crystals; it just takes patience and perseverance. Creating a connection with a crystal ball, an obsidian mirror, or any scrying tool takes time. If what you learned makes no sense, or if you simply feel you received no messages, keep trying. This is a kinship that is taking shape. Like any new relationship, it should not be rushed.

After use, cleanse and recharge your crystal ball periodically. Psychic instruments are personal and should be kept in a safe, private place. Store it by wrapping it in dark-colored material; black velvet or silk is the best choice for housing any crystal used to converse with the Great Unknown.

SPIRIT COMMUNICATION

SPEAKING WITH OUR BELOVED DEAD: MEDIUMSHIP

All that has ever been alive on the earth has been returned to it. Consider that the crystals and gemstones we treasure have been mined among the bones of hundreds of generations of our ancestors. Those of us who communicate with the dead have put these stones to use as valuable tools that solidify an elusive link with those who have crossed over—and you can, too.

The first stone Leanne employed as a medium was a moonstone. It sat on her table at the very first faire she worked. Moonstone has become a popular choice for jewelry, and most places that carry tumbled stones will offer it. The black and red varieties are among the most popular stones at Gallows Hill Witchery, especially in sphere form. It is associated with the moon and its power to illuminate the dark, bringing light to the darkness of death so the living can see past the veil. The stone Sandra relies on most for mediumship work is labradorite, which has likewise long been linked to the spirit world as a bridge that assists the dead in joining the living for contact, closure, and healing.

Working with crystals regularly heightens our psychic gifts, as the vibration of the stones increases the contact from the other side. Holding a **clear quartz crystal** in your hand while meditating on a particular spirit forms a deep relationship with the deceased, amplifying their messages so you can understand what is being communicated. One of Sandra's most prized tools for mediumship is a large clear quartz crystal point that once belonged to Shawn Poirier, and was used by Laurie Cabot during her Speaking to the Dead event as part of the Festival of the Dead in 2019. Now, it resides in Sandra's temple, on the ancestral altar.

CREATING YOUR ANCESTRAL ALTAR

An ancestral altar is a shrine in your temple created to honor your loved ones who have crossed over. It may be simple or elaborate; the choice is yours. There is no right or wrong way to set it up as long as it is done with respect. Choose personal items that reflect the best memories of those whose physical presence is no longer a part of your daily life.

Most of these altars contain images in the form of cherished photographs, but there may be other mementos as well that call to mind the highlights of the lives of those we honor: ticket stubs, challenge coins, medals, dog tags, a favorite mug, a well-worn cap. Items that they enjoyed can also be left as offerings there to encourage their presence, like a favorite candy bar, a pipe, or "the usual" in the form of a cup of coffee or a shot of something even stronger. Incorporating crystals into the shrine can help open the lines of communication. We both have labradorite towers on our ancestral altars, and they form the pillars of the doorway that the spirits of our personal ancestors are welcomed through.

SELF-CARE CRYSTALS FOR PSYCHIC MEDIUMS

Mediums must protect themselves from low vibrations such as fear, anxiety, grief, and regret. Before doing any mediumship work, hold a **smoky quartz** for a light grounding that is not so heavy as to dull the connection to spirit but will counterbalance any harmful energy you encounter.

Lapis lazuli is a potent stone that protects the psychic medium not only from any negativity emanating from the spirit world but also from other spirit workers who may wish them harm. It also enhances psychic power, clairvoyance (visions), and clairaudience (auditory psychic messages). Pair it with **garnet**, which establishes an active barrier that will keep out unwanted energies, awakens higher thinking, and energizes anyone who carries or wears it.

HELLO FROM THE OTHER SIDE

To prepare to open yourself to the spirit world, raise your own vibration first. Depending on your personal beliefs, you may wish to call on angelic forces, such as your guardian angel, or other spirit guides to lead the way safely. Crystals act as a conductor to the presence of your loved ones in spirit. If you're not sure which ones to use, try **angelite** or **celestite**.

Sit in a quiet place where you won't be disturbed.
Take your chosen crystal in your hands and hold it to your heart.

Close your eyes, and ask your guides to watch over you.

Release any tension you are holding in your body. (Scan your jaws, shoulders, hands, and all the way down.)

Focus on the rising and falling of your breath until you can sense its rhythm.

Count backward from ten to one, seeing the numbers in your mind.

Visualize white light bursting from your heart, surrounding you in an aura of protection.

Then, imagine yourself walking along the shore of a beach or a body of water you are familiar with. You recognize someone off in the distance, walking toward you. That is the soul that wishes to speak with you. You may converse, or embrace, or speak your mind as they quietly listen. When it feels right to do so, thank them for spending time with you, and if you want, let them know that this is how you will contact them in the future.

MYSTERIES REVEALED: CRYSTAL SKULLS

As we discussed in chapter 2, crystal skulls have been shrouded in mystery (and controversy) since the latter part of the 1800s. The most famous ones are on display in museums in England and France. Their origin stories and purported powers have inspired fantasy movies, causing some people to write them off entirely as a hoax. Despite some outlandish claims, the most notorious crystal skulls have these key concepts in common:

- Knowledge and wisdom—the stories center on the skulls imparting "universal knowledge and secrets" when humans are "ready" to receive them.

- Healing—the lore includes many tales of curing various ailments and diseases, even cancer.

- Spiritual growth—working with the skulls is believed to enlighten and transform those who are called.

As a skullkeeper, Sandra has experienced all these things with her own Council of Skulls; her largest one, Ivova, is carved from almost five pounds of clear quartz crystal, and her presence has strengthened Sandra's ability to see unhindered pathways of manifestation.

You also read in chapter 2 that the shape of a crystal defines two significant things: the way energy emanates from it passively, and the way energy is transmitted through it actively. Due to their features, skulls are natural communicators. They amplify the psychic gifts of clairvoyance, clairaudience, and clairsentience (psychic "knowing"), facilitating communication with one's higher self, spirits, ancestors, cosmic entities, and more. The carvings themselves are not

SACRED SPACE: CRYSTALS IN THE TEMPLE

ancient, but the minerals they are carved from are, and that's where the power lies.

Is It a Residence or a Doorway?

Some skulls are not meant to house one spirit permanently, meaning that you can open one up as a portal of communication. Think of it like the shell of a hermit crab. A spirit may enter for a short time to convey information or perform a task, and then move on, allowing other spirits to come through when welcomed or summoned. Skulls in a crystal grid communicate information to the practitioner, and their energy can be boosted by a combination of crystals, candles, and other skulls. (To see a crystal skull grid layout, see chapter 12.) If you are called to work with a crystal skull, you'll know it when you feel it. Bring it home, gently cleanse it as you would other crystals, and introduce yourself.

Connecting to Your New Skull

The mineral a skull is carved from emits a certain energy that may attract spirits attuned to that purpose, the same way that you are drawn to certain stones. Sometimes the skull you encounter has a resident spirit that is already present. To find out if yours does, place the first two fingers of your dominant hand in the middle of your forehead (touching what is known as your third eye and a center of your own psychic awareness), and place the first two fingers of your nondominant hand on the same area of the skull's forehead; this is a way to open a line of communication. Do you sense a presence? It may feel the way it does when you answer a phone call and the person on the other end doesn't say anything, but you can tell there's someone on the line; or, you may begin to have a silent conversation in your mind. You also may feel and hear nothing at all . . . It's okay if no-

THE SALEM WITCHES' WAY
TO ACTIVATE YOUR CRYSTAL SKULL

Provide a welcoming space: Place a charging plate, altar pentacle, or similar item from your practice in the center of a circle of crystals. The crystals you choose should carry the vibrations you are hoping to awaken in the skull.

Place a tealight candle at each of the four directions and light them, beginning in the east and moving clockwise.

Touch your wand or the index and middle fingers of your dominant hand to the skull's third eye (in the center of its forehead).

Use your wand or your fingers to awaken the crystals in the outer circle by channeling energy to each one, starting in the east and moving clockwise until all of them have been activated.

Then bring the energy into the center, and touch the skull's third eye again.

body's home! Not every skull has a spirit in residence when you receive it, and you may not wish to invite one. It's perfectly fine to work with the stone's energy without asking anyone to move in.

Once you have awakened your crystal skull, its purpose will become clear to you. Whether it is here to impart wisdom from ancestors or other spirits, heal physical ailments or generational trauma, reveal past-life knowledge, facilitate spiritual growth, or all of the above, it is up to you to maintain the relationship. Making time to meditate with the skull, and feeding it with sacred incense smoke or other offerings, is your responsibility now. Like so many relationships, it takes work to get the results you want.

☀ 10 ☀

FAMILY JEWELS:
FROM PREGNANCY TO PARENTHOOD

Parenthood: the toughest job you'll ever love. We have recommended certain crystals—and ideas to put them to good use,
from boosting fertility to making pregnancy more pleasant (or at least

bearable)—to many hopeful and expectant parents over the years. Working with crystals for those in the family way is hardly "new age." In ancient Egypt, women relied on lapis lazuli to reduce the emotional and physical stress associated with pregnancy and childbirth. To this day, people turn to these ageless methods to relieve pain, discomfort, and fear. We've seen Earth's treasures soothe baby and parent alike, and help growing children face common concerns like nightmares, monsters under the bed, stress from schoolwork, disagreements with peers, bullying, and more.

A Whole New Meaning to "Rocking" the Cradle

Pregnancy is both empowering and exhausting, the birth of a child both thrilling and nerve-wracking. Each stage has emotional, physical, and spiritual challenges, and like others we face in life, crystals and gems can guide us through them.

Pregnant women sometimes experience a heightened sense of spirituality and psychic gifts; we've seen this with many clients over the years. Some expectant parents research the magical properties of crystals, studying the meanings and gifts of each, as they look into ways to aid the process. Others use their intuition to guide them to which crystal would be the best tool in supporting a healthy pregnancy and delivery. Listen to your babies, too; paying attention to their movement when you hold certain stones will tell you which ones to keep on hand to stimulate or soothe them.

Over the past two decades, we've seen many people taking an interest in creating a more natural birthing experience for both mother and child. These crystals help them form a link to Mother Earth, which provides sustenance and strength to both mother and developing child. (Important note: All of these crystals enhance the pregnancy and delivery experiences, but the guidance of a doctor or midwife is, of course, essential.) They can be carried in a charm bag, worn on the body as jewelry, held while meditating, or placed in different rooms of the house, particularly in the nursery—out of baby's reach.

GET IT ON AND KEEP IT GOING: GARNET

Rich, red **garnet** embodies sexual passion and jolts the life-force, restoring the flow of energy and removing blockages to clear the way for fertility. Folk wisdom indicates that garnets are a must: A client of Leanne's carried one in her pocket daily while she was pregnant, for a safe and healthy nine months.

FOR SMOOTH SAILING: AQUAMARINE

Pregnancy may cause nausea, sleeplessness, and headaches, all of which **aquamarine** can help manage. To relieve the physical symptoms of pregnancy, guard against miscarriages and premature labor, and calm your frayed nerves, carry aquamarine or wear it on your wrists or as a pendant on a long chain.

GOODNIGHT, MOON: MOONSTONE

The silvery moon is the Mighty Mother Goddess that watches over us at night, and one of the most important pregnancy stones is **moonstone**, as it is our primary crystal connection to the divine feminine. It can be used in all phases of pregnancy—including the wishing stage. Place a moonstone under your mattress before conception to encourage fertility. **Carry or wear moonstone (especially the red/peach variety) to help with the transition into motherhood.** Tumbled rainbow moonstones may be placed in a warm bath during labor for the blessings of a smooth, successful delivery. While pregnant with her children, Leanne wore a moonstone pendant around her neck to protect her and her babies with great goddess energy.

THE MIDWIVES' SECRET WEAPON: MALACHITE

This beautiful, banded green stone has been used for centuries for all manner of healing; its chemical content can fight infection, reduce inflammation, and bolster the body's natural immune response. **Nicknamed "the midwife stone," malachite is said to ease labor pains and ensure a successful childbirth. Try holding a malachite palm stone or wand in your hand during contractions.**

Nurturing the Bloodline: Red Jasper

This deep-red stone protects and supports the nourishment, growth, and development of the unborn child. To ease pain, increase strength, and boost overall health, place **red jasper** stones directly on the pregnant belly.

Best Before and After: Unakite

Mottled-green/peachy **unakite** brings peace of mind and offers much-needed patience and strength to expectant mothers. Combining both masculine and feminine energies, it calms the central nervous system and brings the body into a state of balance. **Carry or wear unakite for emotional and physical stability during pregnancy and delivery, and to recover from the stress of childbirth.**

Full Circle:
Incorporating Crystals into
the Motherhood Journey

Our friend Amy Hearns is a practicing Witch and initiate of the Celtic Traditionalist Gwyddonaid who spent a good deal of her pregnancy waking up with us on our daily Tea Time Zoom meetings. When she was hoping to grow her family, Amy cast a full moon spell over a jar of fertility tea. Prior to preparing and drinking the tea, she placed a tumbled green aventurine and two large pieces of moonstone on each side of the jar so it would absorb the crystals' energy and be blessed with fertile power as well as the divine feminine force of the Moon and the Goddess.

Every night of her pregnancy, she used a rose quartz beauty roller (which she originally purchased for her skin-care routine) over her growing belly to send her baby loving vibrations. In her third trimester, she started brewing raspberry-leaf sun tea—which helps with uterine toning and eases labor—daily, drinking in the blessings of the Sun for strength and good health. She would place a large heart-shaped carnelian on the pitcher so the tea would absorb its benefits of vitality, keeping her energy up as her body changed.

During the last full moon before baby's due date, she placed a sunstone and a moonstone in the water before brewing, asking for several boons from the God and Goddess: protection and good health for both herself and the baby, and balance in body and mind heading into labor. Amy also put celestite and angelite on the bassinet for their calming, soothing energy and celestial protection.

The pandemic made a traditional baby shower impossible, so as her delivery date approached, Amy asked each of her friends to mail her a small crystal with a hole in it. With these points, she created a "birthing necklace." The idea was to harness all the energies of the women in her life to accompany her during and after labor since no one could physically be there to support her. To the twenty-five crystals she received, she added special charms and stones that belonged to her grandmother and great-grandmother. She went into labor feeling the love of her entire circle embracing her and cheering her on.

On August 6, 2020, healthy and strong Corgan Hearns came into this world surrounded by the love of his parents, the energy of friends and family, and blessings both earthly and divine.

Kids Love Crystals

When it comes to the metaphysical and magical, children take to it like ducks to water. They have not yet become jaded by experience or worried about the opinions of those who already are. Their connection with both the natural and supernatural worlds is powerful and uncorrupted by doubt and disbelief. We have yet to meet a child who wasn't captivated by the bowls and bins of brightly colored crystals and shining stones in our shops. (It is no wonder that the Pet Rock was a huge hit in the 1970s. Although it was seen as a gag gift, we knew people who loved their rock companion. They appreciated the stability and grounding it offered—along with the sense of play and humor.)

ACTIVITY: CRYSTALLIZED INTENTIONS = DEEPER CONNECTIONS

Gather some smooth rocks on a beach or from a local riverbed, or order them online (search for "kindness rocks"). Get acrylic paint pens and inexpensive acrylic paints online or at your local art supply store. Come up with words together that symbolize things that make your child feel happy, safe, and loved. Add words that may be challenges for them, and things they are striving for or need to work on. Paint the rocks in their favorite colors, and write the intention words on them. Place them into a bowl with tumbled stones that offer love, protection, and peace, like rose quartz, black tourmaline, and blue calcite, and use them as a way to check in with your child regularly: Choose one of the rocks to talk about every Sunday night, and then use it as a jumping-off point for conversations during that week.

Unlike other things that are good for them, like toothbrushing and early bedtimes, connecting with crystals is something kids really enjoy. This makes it easy to incorporate them into their routine so they can face any number of challenges. Crystals are not meant to replace medical advice, therapists, or teachers, but they can supplement that official guidance, and they are a fun and effective tool to help children reach their full potential.

It's Not All Fun and Games: Crystals for Growing Pains

The truism gets repeated with every generation: *It is not easy being a kid today.* But there are things that children face now that many of us didn't have to consider, such as the impact of social media, the prevalence of deadly violence in schools, and the lingering damage of a global pandemic. Another persistent problem is bullying. We both dealt with it while we were growing up; our parents and grandparents had stories, too, but it seems to have only gotten worse with every new generation.

Leanne had a client who came into the shop for help for her daughter, who was getting apprehensive each day about attending school, where she was often picked on to the point of tears. The mother was suffering, too, watching her daughter shrink in fear, this once vivacious child losing her confidence and spirit. Leanne chose two stones for her: one, smoky quartz, which would keep her calm, cool, and collected when anyone tried to rattle her, and give her the strength to neutralize any insults they hurled her way instead of internalizing their negativity. The second was tiger's eye, a protective stone that bolsters courage, strength, and self-confidence, creating an impenetrable, invisible armor, and boosting her self-esteem. Leanne encouraged the child to pick a third stone that called to her. She chose a beautiful pink rose quartz. Leanne explained that the crystal knew that she could conquer her fears—and win over or shut down those who were making fun of her. She instructed her to hold the rose quartz near her heart when her feelings were hurt and focus on its loving energy.

FIVE CRYSTALS TO COMBAT BULLYING

Smoky quartz—dissolves fear, neutralizes negativity

Tiger's eye—imparts courage, encourages problem solving/ creative solutions

Black tourmaline—transmutes negativity into fuel to overcome challenges

Hematite—stabilizes and enhances feelings of security

Ruby—builds confidence and self-esteem

Six months later, the mother-and-daughter team returned to the shop to see Leanne. The little girl was much more confident and outspoken, and proudly reported that the kids who had been picking on her had backed down. This wise child was now able to control her own emotions when faced with the others' negativity and had even made new friends. She was no longer afraid to walk into school every day, and—other than too much homework—she had no big complaints.

Leanne reads for a special education teacher who has given some of her students **blue lace agate** to assist with communication and expression. Simply carrying a tumbled blue lace agate in your pocket brings a sense of peace and is an effective "worry stone" to fiddle with

---

FIVE CRYSTALS TO HELP WITH
FOCUS AT SCHOOL AND BEYOND

Fluorite—enhances mental stability and self-discipline

Lepidolite—supports emotional healing and balance

Carnelian—replenishes inspiration, passion for learning

Citrine—ignites creativity and mental clarity

Howlite—quiets an overactive imagination

---

when anxious. It is especially helpful to children who get nervous when speaking in front of the class or performing for a crowd.

Neither of us had any issues speaking in front of the class; in fact, we were both guilty of talking too much at school. Leanne was mocked by teachers who didn't understand why she had a hard time staying focused. She was a good student, so she wasn't diagnosed with ADHD until she was an adult, and her children were facing the same issues. They were given medication, but Leanne felt that it basically turned them into zombies. If she could go back in time, she would try using some of the crystals she has gotten to know in the years since, like lepidolite and fluorite, to help with their attention span, focus, and mood. These stone allies have helped her keep her own ADHD symptoms in check.

"Go the F*** to Sleep!": Crystals for a Better Bedtime

Everyone needs sleep, and everyone gets tired, but no one knows sleep deprivation better than new parents, and it is often years before their sleep patterns recover. First, it's the late-night feedings. Then, it's the middle-of-the-night shenanigans, or the "can I come sleep with you?" visits, or the "just one more story" requests. Children's brains are so creative and inquisitive, they don't seem to ever shut off.

AMETHYST AMBIENCE

To set a snooze mood, place an **amethyst** tower on an LED light base to function as a high-vibration nightlight. Bonus: It'll cut down on bad dreams.

SELENITE SERENITY

To help a child who is suffering from any type of illness get a better night's rest, place a piece of **selenite** under their mattress. Selenite recharges the body and mind, promoting a health-giving sleep. It is also known as "liquid light" because its cleansing, purifying aura helps

---

FIVE CRYSTALS THAT "ROCK" CHILDREN TO SLEEP

Sodalite—instills harmony, gives off a peaceful vibe

Howlite—soothes intense emotions, quiets the mind

Amethyst—calms the psychic mind, promotes a deeper connection with dream states

Moonstone—reduces worry, stops racing thoughts

Selenite—resets energy and improves the quality of sleep

---

with deep and undisturbed slumber. Selenite candle holders will also form a peaceful sleep space; use a battery-powered tealight instead of a flame for safety.

Banish Bad Dreams

Children are naturally psychic and open to spirit. That receptivity means they absorb a lot of psychic information during each day, which can include overwhelming emotions, stress, and anxiety. This can manifest itself as nightmares. Placing crystal guardians in the form of towers or spheres can help (see the suggested list on the previous page). We have also found it helpful to involve children in the creation of a special "Nightmare Begone" spray to banish bad dreams and safeguard everyone's sanity.

Nightmare Begone Spray

If your child is connecting with spirits at night and struggling with sleep, make this spray with crystals and essential oils to chase away all negativity and put talkative spirits to rest, so you can, too.

You need:
8-ounce spray bottle
¾ cup distilled water

3 drops essential lavender oil

5 drops essential frankincense oil

1 teaspoon rose quartz chips or 1 tumbled rose quartz

1 teaspoon amethyst chips or 1 tumbled amethyst

Optional: 1 teaspoon glitter

Put all ingredients in the bottle. Shake up and spray into the air around the sleeping area.

ROCK OF AGES, STILL ROLLING . . .

Sandra still works with the first stone she was ever gifted: a piece of fossilized coral given to her by her father. It sits in her temple in a shell bowl in the west, on the altar honoring the element of Water. That crystal has accompanied her through dozens of moves and countless life changes. This ancient stone links us to the wisdom of the ages, so it is fitting that it is the oldest in her personal collection. Holding it brings her back to the good days of her childhood, and it has helped her heal some of the trauma she experienced.

Humans have picked up rocks and collected them since they were first used as tools in prehistoric times. It is as if the Earth Mother has always reached out to us in the hopes that we will get to know Her, love Her, and protect Her, thereby safeguarding our own survival. Teaching the children in your life about stones will help them grow, overcome life's obstacles, and teach them that we are all connected to the earth, and one another. We all deserve to be honored and respected for our unique gifts.

✳11✳

BEST FRIEND VIBES:
CRYSTALS AND OUR FUR FAMILIES

As so many forms of Witchcraft are tied to the cycles of nature, Witches are known to have a special relationship with animals—both wild and tame—and a quick review of witchy social media reveals that we clearly love our companion creatures. Witch and non-Witch alike, many of us have "fur kids," and we would be lost without them.

Animals are connected to the inner workings of the world around them, so attuning to them, communicating with them, and sending them healing energy with the help of Earth's jewels seems like a no-brainer. As long as you take extra care in your methods, crystals can help you bond with your four-legged, finned, and feathered friends in a variety of ways.

You may have heard that many Witches have familiars: spirit guides who have taken the form of an animal on Earth. They are pets that connect to us at a soul level, imparting wisdom and acting as guards and guides on this plane and beyond, whether they're cats or dogs, snakes or rabbits, horses, goats, parrots, doves, beta fish, toads, scorpions, or tarantulas. Though these animals are each unique, the bond is the same, and it can be initiated and nurtured with the assistance of crystals.

ANIMAL ATTUNEMENT: LEOPARD SKIN JASPER

Leopard skin jasper, also known as "the jaguar stone," connects people to their animals on a profound level by creating a link in the spiritual plane, as well as an aura in the physical plane. Place a large

A NOTE OF CAUTION

When working with animals, the size and location of a crystal must be carefully considered. In general, we don't recommend that your pets have unsupervised contact with any of your stones. Small crystals should be used with the greatest care, as we don't want our fur friends to swallow them. One way to use crystals with your pets is to infuse their diet with crystal energy, but you should never place the stones in the food. Instead, imbue a meal with the power of a stone by placing it into the empty bowl temporarily (such as overnight) in a location your pet cannot access (such as inside a cabinet or closet), then removing it prior to offering food. If you use crystal-infused water with your pet, be sure to research the stones you are using to confirm they are safe for animals. The following common crystals are not recommended for direct use with pets due to their toxicity if swallowed:

apatite	citrine	malachite
aragonite	fluorite	pyrite
azurite	jet	scolecite

tower (or a sphere too large to fit in your pet's mouth) of leopard skin jasper near the pet's sleeping area to create and support an atmosphere of mutual understanding.

CREATURE COMFORTS:
OBSIDIAN AND SODALITE

When Leanne's friend Carol first adopted her dog Jellybean, she used crystals to calm and emotionally heal her new friend. Jellybean was a traumatized shelter rescue. She was afraid of people, especially men, and when she encountered strangers, she would shake uncontrollably. Carol carefully sewed a **black obsidian** into the lining of Jellybean's collar, which diminishes feelings of loneliness and anxiety in dogs and puts animals at ease, giving them a sense of confidence in their surroundings. Black obsidian will also protect animals and bring comfort when they are separated from their person. Today, Jellybean is a well-adjusted dog, loving her forever home and her humans. If you're not handy with a sewing needle, try patting your pet while holding an obsidian palm stone or wand in the other hand; you can try massaging them lightly with the stone, too. Place a large tower or sphere in their area—but out of reach—to reap the same benefits while you are not present.

Animals can experience bouts of anxiety and nervousness just like us. One stone that works well to restore harmony and promote relaxation for the whole pack is **sodalite**. A tower or sphere placed near the entrance can calm the "someone's here" craziness that happens when visitors step through the door. Try using a wand or palm stone when patting your pets to soothe them. Sodalite generates a peaceful vibration that helps facilitate nonverbal communication between pets and their owners, so it's perfect for new furry friends because it opens up trust and restores spiritual balance. Sodalite's healing properties can encourage nervous dogs and cats to be more social, by supporting their emotional balance so they experience less fear.

MORE THAN JUST PUPPY LOVE: ROSE QUARTZ

Rose quartz is known for its romantic powers, but it also supports the unconditional love we experience with our animals. This crystal can build a loving bond between pets and owners, and is particularly useful when adopting an adult animal with a traumatic past. It is also associated with physical heart health and circulation, so you can share these benefits with your new BFF (Best Fur Friend) by wearing matching rose quartz: a pendant or ring for you, and a collar charm if your pet can wear one. They will feel your love all day even if you have to be apart.

CALMING THE WATERS: AQUAMARINE

With its wonderfully soothing energy, this blue or blue-green stone can bring peace between all creatures, from fur to fins. Its name means "water of the sea," and it radiates the healing power of the element of Water. Folklore says that these stones first belonged to mermaids and could protect sailors from the perils of the ocean. If you plan to travel anywhere near water with your pet, tuck an **aquamarine** into the pocket of their carrier, or in a charm bag tied to the handle. If your pet or familiar is aquatic, this is your best choice for changes and transitions. When introducing new fish to your fin family, first charge the water by touching it with an aquamarine crystal, and keep it near the tank to create harmony between the dwellers.

Leanne's daughter, Elizabeth, adores her pet turtle, Small Fry, whose tank is filled with an array of crystals and jasper stones. Small Fry gravitates toward the clear crystal quartz in particular, which is located directly on his heating stone and helps keep him strong and healthy. Clear quartz also helps Elizabeth to connect on an emotional level with her beloved turtle.

HARMONY IN THE DEN:
ANIMAL BONDING CHARM BAG

Introducing new animals to an established fur family is rarely an easy task. Our friend and fellow Tea Timer Amy Hearns owns animals of all kinds—everything from sugar gliders to hedgehogs. When her friend rescued two cats, they kept fighting with each other. She took brushings of fur from each of the two cats and entwined them with catnip, a rose quartz tumbled stone, and a selenite and placed them into a charm bag near their beds (but out of their reach) to create a soothing vibration. Within hours, the catfights stopped. Today these kitty siblings snuggle together in peace. When bringing an animal into the fold, you can create a similar charm bag; if you use catnip, be sure to hang it where the cats can't get into it! Envision the soft-pink and white aura of the stones surrounding the animals, radiating good vibes and creating a safe space to relax into their new routine.

Bright-Eyed and Bushy-Tailed: Crystals and Pet Health

When animals get sick or are experiencing discomfort, pet parents often feel powerless to help. We wish we could speak the same language so they could tell us what's wrong. Working with stones and crystals can improve a condition, but of course it is by no means a replacement for a properly trained veterinarian; it is simply another measure that can be added to a trained professional's recommendation by amplifying healing energy, reducing panic, and boosting vitality and strength to pets and owners alike.

When Leanne's magical dog niece Kiah became mysteriously sick, it caused a great amount of concern within the pup's extended family. Her dog moms, Amanda and Jessie, were frantic, and called Leanne for emotional and magical support on their way to the emergency veterinary hospital, explaining that Kiah had abruptly begun exhibiting unusual behavior patterns that she had never shown before. Leanne called Sandra, and they both got to work. Leanne focused on her carnelian tower coupled with a red spell candle to restore vitality and drive in Kiah. She wrote Kiah's name on parchment paper, along with her sister and mommas' names, sending them each strength and courage. Not only is carnelian associated with those traits, but it has also been used to help resolve neurological issues, which Kiah appeared to be suffering from. Sandra made an appeal to Sekhmet, an Egyptian goddess she has worked with for many years for human as well as animal healing; she placed her basalt statue of Sekhmet in the center of a ring of clear quartz crystals with a blue calcite wand, a carnelian palm stone, a piece of jade, and a jackal carved out of tiger's eye at the four quarters of the circle (east, south, west, and north). With the help of an amazing emergency veterinarian, Kiah is now recovering and back to her energetic self.

Speaking of amazing veterinarians, Dr. Leslie Siewko is our official pet doctor of choice, and at Our Family Veterinary Services, she has placed a number of crystals from Sandra's company, Gallows Hill Witchery, around the clinic to help the animals in her top-notch care. In the front of the office, sodalite, tourmaline, and shungite set the atmosphere for both humans and animals, offering peace, harmony, grounding, and electromagnetic field protection from the high-tech electronics in the suite. In the recovery room, every cage is adorned with its own crystal amulet created by the resident animal acupuncturist. Dr. Leslie has seen improvements in the attitude of patients as well as staff since introducing crystals into the practice.

To cut down on the usual anxiety surrounding planned checkups, place **dalmatian jasper, turquoise,** and **blue calcite** tumbled stones into a white charm bag for enhanced communication, healing, and tranquility. Hold the charm bag to activate it for a few minutes before tying it to the carrier, or if you are using a leash, tuck it into a waste-bag dispenser that attaches near the handle.

To ward off unwanted trips to the vet, "Master Healers" **clear quartz** and **amethyst** can be programmed with intention through meditation. Find a private, comfortable spot to sit. If your pet will sit with you, even better. Hold a clear quartz in your dominant hand and an amethyst in the other, and close your eyes, drawing in nine deep breaths, each time exhaling with purpose. Visualize your pet being surrounded in rays of healing light in bands of opalescent color. After each breath, you may choose to speak aloud, or think to yourself, a word or simple phrase that encompasses your desire for your pet's health, such as *flexibility*, *vitality*, *long happy life*, or similar goals. Sit for as long as it takes to feel the shift in energy (it may be three minutes or ten), then place the crystals in a safe spot out of your pet's reach where you can see them, and revisit this exercise once a week. We like to do this exercise on Sundays, for the blessings of the planet that governs all living creatures here on Earth.

BETTER BELLY RUBS AND SNOOT BOOPS WITH CRYSTALS

Rubbing an animal with crystals offers both emotional strength and physical benefits. It can also create a meaningful link between animals and their human parents. But massaging a pet depends on the animal—a frisky cat probably won't want to be restrained or even sit still to be loved without their consent. Temperament is your guide here.

Leanne's fur child, Sadie, has a tiger's eye adhered safely to her collar for protection and strength. Sadie is sensitive to the energy fields around even the most passive crystals in the house: She gets the zoomies around carnelian, while moonstone helps her sleep. In particular she loves to have her belly rubbed with a rose quartz palm stone. Leanne believes it intensifies their bond.

As pets age and their energy diminishes, they get progressively more sluggish. They can also become stiffer and have difficulty getting around due to arthritis and muscle atrophy. Abigail, Sandra's elderly pug, was noticeably more flexible after three things: a daily treat that contains glucosamine and chondroitin, regular stretching of her back legs, and the addition of several large clear quartz towers into the room she spends the most time in.

Additional stones that play well with animals:

Black tourmaline can help animals adapt to new environments. It regulates moods and protects our empathic pets from the fallout of our own negative emotions. Black tourmaline rubbed on a pet's belly can assist with digestive discomforts and stimulate the appetite of picky eaters.

Amber can be rubbed on your aging pet's head for increased energy and to help calm their fears. Amber is said to hold ancient wisdom that can benefit all walks of life, and can encourage animals to learn quickly, whether they are attending puppy or K9 school, training to be emotional support or service animals, or being taught some cool tricks.

Moss agate is the crystal equivalent of a thunder shirt or weighted blanket for animals. Its earthy energy will help your pet settle down. Like the cool moss it is named after, moss agate gives off relaxing and grounding vibes that both you and your pets will appreciate in times of stress.

12

THE PATTERNS OF MAGIC: CRYSTAL GRIDS

The process of creating a crystal grid is another form of meditation and can be a deeply personal, sacred act. There is no right or wrong way to create one. There are dozens of templates online, which you can use as jumping-off points, but the real magic happens when you allow your creativity and intuition to guide your design.

You may wish to play some music that sets the tone, whatever that means to you. Once you have assembled the grid, sit with it and try insight meditation, or use the center item as your focus for concentration meditation.

Here are our time-tested layouts. Hopefully they will inspire you to bring your own to life.

The Four Quarters Grid

Grounding and Centering, Balance, Healing, Self-Care, and Inner Work

The equal-armed cross within the circle is a symbol for planet Earth and is the basis of the Native American medicine wheel.

In the middle, place a crystal sphere that is associated with the focus of your spell.

In the east, a feather.

In the south, a tealight candle.

In the west, a small bowl of water.

In the north, a septarian egg, or a similar stone that represents stability and grounding.

Form the circle with other stones and crystals that support the work (see the glossary for guidance).

THE PENTAGRAM GRID

PROTECTION AND MANIFESTATION MAGIC

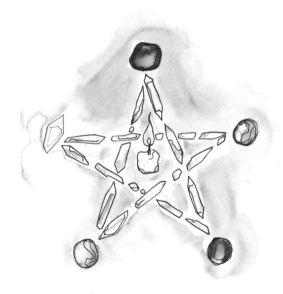

The five-pointed star is a symbol that has transformed through the centuries; for us, it is a dynamic, protective glyph that represents the five sacred elements: Earth, Fire, Air, Water, and Spirit. This grid can be used to manifest a variety of results, from career and financial dreams to relationship goals, as well as to send energy to loved ones for health, protection, and other blessings. In this case, place a photo, memento, or other similar object link to the recipient in the center with the candle.

Lay out crystal points or tumbled stones to form a star.

Place a purple stone (like amethyst) at the topmost point, indicating Spirit.

A blue stone (like blue calcite or blue lace agate) at the point of the upper-right arm, for Water.

A red stone (like garnet or carnelian) at the point of the lower-right arm, to symbolize Fire.

A green stone (like aventurine or malachite) at the point of the lower-left arm, for Earth.

A yellow stone (like citrine or lemon quartz) at the point of the upper-left arm, to represent Air.

Place a spell candle that you have anointed and charged in the center, and light it, speaking the words of the spell, or from your heart. To charge a candle for a specific spell, use an active method, such as holding the candle between your palms and focusing your intent on it. If you can focus and feel your energy, you can charge a candle. Our book *Lighting the Wick* contains step-by-step instructions for making them, or you can purchase prepared ones online.

VESICA PISCIS GRID

COMBINATION, COLLABORATION, AND COOPERATION

The vesica piscis is the foundation of two popular crystal grid patterns, the Seed of Life and the Flower of Life. This shape honors the combination of two things, whether that's joining forces with a partner on a project, linking up with a lover, or envisioning yourself in a position you have applied for. This is about unity as well as the protection of that coupling.

In one circle, place the stones you identify with: your birthstone, a crystal you have carried with you for a long time, a favorite gemstone pendant, or all of these. In the other circle, place the crystals and stones that represent what you are drawing in. You may choose to draw the "eye" on a piece of paper in the center of the two circles, which protects your desire from the Evil Eye, or jealous gaze of others. If you have crystals that can form the image of the eye, use those; you could also use beads, glass fish tank pebbles, or other items to form the eye. (See the vesica piscis artwork for inspiration.) You may also place a spell candle prepared for your purpose in the center of the eye.

CRYSTAL SKULL GRID

ANCESTOR VENERATION, SPIRIT COMMUNICATION

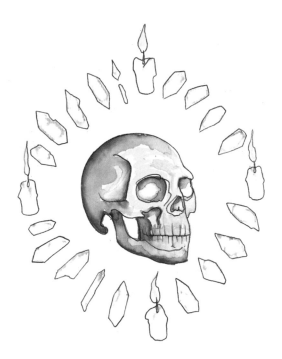

In chapter 9, we discussed how to awaken your crystal skull. This grid can be used for the activation, or to communicate with someone who has crossed over or with other entities in the spirit world.

Place your crystal skull in the center of a ring of crystals, with a candle at each of the four directions. You may line crystals up into the four directions as well, calling to mind the four earthly elements, with Spirit represented by the skull.

TO MAKE CONTACT WITH A SPIRIT
THROUGH YOUR CRYSTAL SKULL

Touch the skull's third eye at the center of its forehead with the index and middle fingers of your dominant hand, and speak the name of the spirit you wish to contact. Beginning in the east and working your way around the circle clockwise, light each candle. Then touch the skull's third eye again, and say, "Welcome, [name of spirit]." Conduct your conversation, and when it feels right, bid the spirit goodbye by reversing the steps.

ACKNOWLEDGMENTS

From both of us:

Joy Tutela, we have made our "crystal vision" a reality in this, our third book. Thank you for your continued wise counsel.

Nina Shield, Hannah Steigmeyer, LeeAnn Pemberton, Laura Corless, Jess Morphew, Danielle Deschenes, Farin Schlussel, Carla Iannone, Alyssa Adler, Marian Lizzi, Anne Kosmoski, Megan Newman, and the entire TarcherPerigee/Penguin Random House team, we continue to be blessed with your efforts on our behalf.

Lisa Ainsworth, you're truly in your element with these gorgeous watercolors. Thank you so much for continuing this journey with us.

To all the owners and buyers of stores carrying *Reading the Leaves* and *Lighting the Wick*, and all the readers who purchased them, this latest book is here because you believed in us. We will be forever grateful.

To the Gods!

From Sandra:

Kevin, ours is "no ordinary love." It truly is a fortified foundation, and I love everything we have built, and everything we are building upon it. Thank you for supporting me in all my endeavors.

Mikki, thank you for being my plus one. Your help at the Gallows Hill Witchery booth was invaluable, but what I'm most grateful for is the time we spent, and the open and honest communication we enjoyed. Bitches of Eastwick for life. LYLAS, B!

Thank you to every member of the Gallows Hill Witchery Crystal Coven. Our "Saturday Night Lives" and "Sunday Fundays" give me life. You all rock! ☺

Leanne, the third time is indeed the charm. We continue to Break the Box. I eagerly await our next adventure. Love you!

From Leanne:

Elizabeth and Kevin, my loves and laughter. I am proud of you both. Never forget that family is everything. Always love each other.

Chris, thank you for being my love. You have been my source of joy and peace. Never forget how magnificent you are.

Sadie, my love and life. Oh, Puppy Face, Cheese Doodle dog, the gods blessed me when you came into my life. Thank you for giving me unconditional love.

Amanda, you have been my rock. Thank you for lifting my confidence and helping me find my words. May we always share our morning coffee, magick, and friendship. Love you.

Kiah, your exuberant spirit and love lives on. You were one remarkable dog. I still have a crystal for you on my altar.

Carol, I am blessed to call you friend and family. Thank you for sharing your fur baby stories with me. Our friendship will always be a loving anchor in my stormy life.

Linda Davis, your knowledge and information is weaved into the pages of this book. Much love to my "nephews" Dylan and Dakota, it has been a joy watching you both growing up with crystals in your pockets. You both taught me a great deal.

Amy Hearns, thank you for sharing your stories with us. Love and blessings to you and Corgan.

And to the staff at Pentagram, thank you for all the support while writing this book and promoting all of my magickal and business endeavors.

Pooh Bear, I knew crystals would sell. Your love for this planet and all that lives on it is a testament to your faith. Love, Piglet. "You don't think that's funny? I thought that was very funny."

Sandra, thank you for the gifts of friendship and partnership. Working with you is always a magickal journey. You stuck by me during the dark and the light. You celebrate my success and encourage me to shine. I love you. I look forward to the next loud noise we shall make in the universe.

	CRYSTALS	COLOR	DAY OF THE WEEK
Anger (to Reduce)	Blue calcite, Lepidolite, Smoky quartz, and Shungite	Black and White	Monday
Animal Bonding	Kambaba jasper, Leopard skin jasper, Obsidian, and Sodalite	Brown	Friday
Animal Healing	Blue calcite, Carnelian, Sodalite, and Shungite	Green, Orange	Friday, Wednesday
Animal Protection	Amber, Black tourmaline, and Moss agate	Black, Brown, Red	Tuesday, Friday
Banish Negativity	Black tourmaline, Black obsidian, Jet, and Selenite	Any color	Saturday
Business	Citrine, Carnelian, and Lodestone	Green, Gold	Friday, Sunday
Career	Aventurine, Bloodstone, and Pyrite	Royal blue and Gold	Thursday and Sunday
Communication with Angels/ Spirit Guides	Celestite, Jet, Lapis lazuli, and Iolite	Light blue and Purple	Monday
Creativity	Carnelian, Citrine, and Malachite	Orange	Wednesday
Divination	Clear crystal quartz, Lapis lazuli, and Rose quartz	Purple and Silver	Monday and Saturday
Dreams	Amethyst, Epidote, Lapis lazuli	Purple	Monday
Education	Citrine, Fluorite, Hematite, Zebra jasper	Blue, Orange	Thursday, Wednesday
Emotional Healing	Black tourmaline, Larimar, Fancy jasper, Smoky quartz, and Shungite	Black and White	Saturday
Entertaining	Aquamarine, Chrysocolla, and Citrine	Yellow and Blue	Sunday
Family Fun	Rose quartz, Sodalite, Rainbow moonstone, and Banded brown aragonite	Pink, Green, and Silver	Day of the activity

OIL	HERB	CUISINE	PLANET
Lavender	Calendula, Sea salt	Watermelon and Strawberries	Mercury and Venus
Vanilla	Rose, Rosemary	Pumpkin	Venus
Rosemary	Frankincense and Myrrh	Food recommended by your vet	Mercury and Venus
Sage	Cedarwood	Food recommended by your vet	Mars and Venus
Rue	Sage	Coffee	Saturn
Allspice, Basil	Bay leaf, Patchouli	Grapes, Peaches	Venus and Sun
Bergamot, Calamus, Cinnamon	Agrimony, Nutmeg, Pine	Hot salsa	Mars and Sun
Frankincense, Myrrh	Angelica, Lavender	Ice cream	Moon
Bergamot	Lavender	Celery, Broccoli	Mercury
Lavender	Frankincense and Myrrh	Coffee, Dark chocolate	Moon and Saturn
Mugwort	Lavender	Milk	Moon
Citrus	Lemon balm	Orange juice	Mercury
Lavender	Cedarwood	Cabbage	Saturn
Lemon and Rose	Rose, Vanilla, and Rosemary	Chili, Salsa	Sun
Sage	Rosemary	Orange sherbet	Sun

	CRYSTALS	COLOR	DAY OF THE WEEK
Fertility	Apatite, Carnelian, Pink calcite, and Garnet	Orange, Pink, and Red	Friday
Friendship	Aventurine, Amethyst, Rose quartz, and Citrine	Green and Pink	Friday
Getting Over a Breakup	Amazonite, Botswana agate, Grossularite, and Malachite	Black, Red	Tuesday, Saturday
Grief	Apatite, Botswana agate, Malachite, and Rhodonite,	Black and White	Saturday
Happiness	Citrine, Lepidolite, and Opalite	Yellow	Sunday
Love	Rose quartz, Peridot, and Jade	Green, Pink	Friday
Luck	Aventurine, Citrine, Lemon topaz, Jade, and Pyrite	Gold, Green	Friday or Saturday
Manifestation	Chalcopyrite, Clear quartz, and Hematoid quartz	Gold, Green, Yellow, Royal blue	Thursday and Sunday
Money	Aventurine, Citrine, Peridot, Pyrite, and Malachite	Gold, Green	Friday or Sunday
Negativity	Anyolite, Black kyanite, Black onyx, and Green kyanite	Black, White	Saturday
Nightmares	Black tourmaline, Green jade, Smoky quartz, and Tiger's eye	White	Monday or Saturday
Plants	Bloodstone and Moss agate	Green	Friday
Pregnancy	Garnet, Aquamarine, Moonstone, Malachite, and Red jasper	Silver, Green	Monday and Friday
Protection	Black tourmaline, Desert rose, Fossil coral, Obsidian, and Jet	Red and Black	Tuesday and Saturday
Psychic Ability	Amethyst, Dumortierite, and Moonstone	Purple or Silver	Monday
Sex	Dragon's blood jasper, Garnet, Red jasper, and Rose quartz	Red or Green	Tuesday or Friday

OIL	HERB	CUISINE	PLANET
Vanilla	Rose and Cinnamon	Chocolate	Venus and Mercury
Lemon, Passion flower, Sweet pea	Lemon, Mullein, Pink roses	Sweet potato pie	Venus and Sun
Black pepper	Sage, Rosemary	Red meat, Onions	Mars
Frankincense	Bay Laurel, Cypress, Tobacco	Pickles, Mustard	Saturn
Apple, Honeysuckle	Basil, Rose	Honey buns	Sun, Venus
Bergamot, Ylang ylang	Basil, Calendula, Oregano, Rose	Honey, Pesto sauce	Venus
Sage	Bay leaf	Nutmeg	Venus, Sun
Bergamot, Orange	Basil, Chamomile, Nutmeg	Butter	Jupiter, Sun
Clove	Cinnamon	Citrus fruit	Venus, Sun
Sage	Sage, Rosemary	Garlic	Saturn
Rosemary, Lavender	Anise	Chamomile tea	Moon, Saturn
Rose	Marjoram	Apple peels	Venus
Lavender, Sandalwood	Fenugreek, Ginger, Rosehip	Grapefruit, Eggs	Moon, Venus
Cedarwood, Juniper, Rosemary	Lavender, Palo santo, Sage	Olive oil, Garlic	Mars and Saturn
Lavender, Frankincense	Myrrh, Lavender, Nutmeg	Lavender lemonade	Monday
Clove Oil	Cinnamon, Ginger	Chai tea	Mars and Venus

	CRYSTALS	COLOR	DAY OF THE WEEK
Sleep	Kunzite, Fluorite, Malachite, Amazonite, Lapis lazuli	Silver or White	Monday
Spirit Communication	Angelite, Garnet, Labradorite, Lapis lazuli, Smoky quartz	Black, Purple, or Silver	Saturday
Strength	Feather agate, Tiger's eye, and Garnet	Red	Tuesday
TRAVEL			
By Land	Amethyst, Hematite, Selenite, and Citrine	Brown	Wednesday
By Air	Blue calcite, Malachite, and Moonstone	Yellow	Wednesday
By Sea	Jasper, Ocean jasper, and Aquamarine	Blue	Wednesday
Weight Loss	Amethyst, Moonstone, and White howlite	Black, Green, White	Monday, Friday, Saturday
ZODIAC			
Aries	Carnelian and Red jasper	Red	Tuesday
Taurus	Aventurine and Emerald	Green	Friday
Gemini	Alexandrite or Chrysocolla	Orange	Wednesday
Cancer	Moonstone or Pearls	Silver	Monday
Leo	Tiger's eye and Pyrite	Gold	Sunday
Virgo	Fluorite and Sapphire	Yellow and Brown	Wednesday
Libra	Pink tourmaline and Opal	Yellow	Friday
Scorpio	Labradorite and Smoky quartz	Red	Tuesday
Sagittarius	Citrine and Turquoise	Blue	Thursday
Capricorn	Garnet and Jet	Dark gray and Blue	Saturday
Aquarius	Amethyst and Celestite	Violet and Blue	Saturday
Pisces	Aquamarine and Blue lace agate	Aquamarine	Thursday

OIL	HERB	CUISINE	PLANET
Lavender	Lavender, Mugwort, Valerian	Chamomile tea	Moon
Mugwort	Wormwood	Pomegranate	Saturn
Sandalwood, Frankincense	Camphor, Mint	Red lentils	Mars
Bergamot	Frankincense	Mint tea	Mercury
Lavender	Copal	Whiskey, Lavender tea	Mercury
Jasmine	Lilac	Glass of water	Mercury
Mugwort	Sea salt	Salad	Moon, Venus, Saturn
Mugwort	Mistletoe	Salsa and chips	Mars
Rose	Thyme	Chocolate-covered strawberries	Venus
Lavender	Lemon balm	Sandwiches	Mercury
Peppermint	Honeysuckle	Ice cream	Moon
Lemon	St. John's wort	Sunflower seeds	Sun
Rosemary	Skullcap	Celery, Carrots	Mercury
Dill	Juniper	Strawberries	Venus
Gardenia	Wormwood	Raspberry jam	Mars
Frankincense	Agrimony	Ginger snap cookies	Jupiter
Comfrey	Rue	Spinach	Saturn
Chamomile	Catnip	Ocean fish	Saturn
Myrrh	Mugwort	Oysters, Whole grains	Jupiter

GLOSSARY

This list comprises the crystals and stones with which we have personally had success. Any of them can be carried, worn as jewelry, placed in your home, used in crystal grids, and more. We've also included recommendations for the most appropriate color charm bags, along with suggestions for the most fruitful intentions and purposes to set.

Amazonite—you want calm, cool, collected energy? This Xanax of crystals is your huckleberry. If you're walking into a high-stress situation, make sure you have amazonite on board, and *pow*—positivity, confidence, and no more knots in your stomach. It can also bring good luck, so add to a gold charm bag when gambling and playing games of chance.

Amber—one of the first materials used in amulets, amber is not technically a stone but rather hardened resin from a tree that has since gone extinct. Add it to a yellow or gold charm bag to energize any spell for increase, growth, and expansion.

Amethyst—millennia-old lore calls amethyst a powerful healer for all manner of ills. In particular, it is associated with sobriety and breaking bad habits: ancient Greeks and Romans believed it could "cure" drunkenness, up to and including relief from a hangover. Amethyst is a direct line to your intuition as well, which is why you see it on the table of many psychics. Negativity does not stand a chance around this queen of crystals, and it promotes relaxation, so keep one on your nightstand or the edge of the tub when you want to soak the day away. Add to a lavender charm bag for prophetic dreams, sobriety support, and enhanced psychic power.

Ametrine—the dynamic duo of amethyst and citrine has characteristics of both. Add to a purple charm bag to combine psychic wisdom and creativity for big ideas.

Angelite—this is one of the best crystals to connect you with angelic forces. Add to a lavender charm bag for heightened awareness and inner peace.

Anyolite (Ruby in Zoisite)—think of it like Lysol for the soul. Add to a white charm bag to repel and block negativity, cleanse and purify a space, and jump-start renewal.

Apatite—brings balance to the mind, body, and soul. Add to a white charm bag to ease sorrow, and bring comfort to the grieving.

Aquamarine—one of the best stones for connecting with the element of Water. Add to a blue charm bag for healing, psychic awareness, peace, and ocean magic.

Aragonite—harnesses the stabilizing power of the earth. Add to a green charm bag to draw upon the energies of the Earth Goddess.

Aventurine—aventurine is especially powerful for healing, but it has many uses. Add to a green charm bag when gambling, for good luck, to invite in fortune and prosperity, and for all varieties of healing.

Axinite—bring in axinite when you need to connect with the spirit of Mother Earth and draw on Her power. Add to a red charm bag for endurance, strength, and courage in times of turmoil.

Banded Agate—when you feel out of sorts, banded agate can supply a much-needed alignment shift. Add to a white charm bag to restore balance and heal the mind, body, and spirit.

Black Kyanite—Sandra calls this "the Witches' broom" because it sweeps away negativity from your aura. Add to a black charm bag to shield you from draining energies, or connect you to past-life memories.

Black Onyx—one of the strongest stones to combat negativity, black onyx is like a black hole that sucks up all the foul energy it encounters—which is why it needs to be cleansed often. (See chapter 2 for instructions.) Add to a black charm bag for protection and defensive magic.

Black Tourmaline—black tourmaline, which is one of Sandra's top three grounding stones, transmutes negative energy into fuel for your own use. Add to a black charm bag to increase physical vitality and grounding.

Bloodstone—awakens the warrior within. A powerful purifier and protector, bloodstone is an excellent addition to any defensive spell or ward. Add to a brown charm bag for strength and courage (especially when facing mortality), and success in agriculture.

Blue Kyanite—one of the only crystals that never requires cleansing; in fact, it cleans the other stones around it. Add to any charm bag to keep all other crystals clear of negativity.

Blue Lace Agate—the intricate patterns seen in these gorgeous stones echo the seafoam that rolls in with the ocean tides, and put forth major soothing vibes. Add to a blue charm bag to bring calm to a situation, or honor the water deities.

Blue Onyx—cool, glossy pools of azure, blue onyx alleviates worry and calms nerves. Add to a purple charm bag to connect with your higher self and spirit guides.

Blue Topaz—this stone is a master de-escalator. Add to a pink charm bag to reconcile with a love, or a blue charm bag for healing.

Botswana Agate—for strong support in times of transition, keep this stone by your side. Add to a white charm bag to ease grief or heal a broken heart.

Bumble Bee Jasper—add to a gold charm bag to enhance your motivation and willpower. Note: Exercise caution when handling, especially if unpolished, as it contains sulfur and arsenic. Keep it away from pets and children.

Carnelian—need to power through some shit? Carnelian is the stone you want in your pocket, on your desk, or around your neck where it can amplify your voice as you speak your truth. Carnelian is the life coach of the mineral world, your Monday Motivation, your kick in the ass on Tuesday, and your leg up over the hump on Wednesday, too. It's about igniting your creativity, fueling your passions, crushing your goals, and manifesting your dreams. BOOM.

Add to a gold charm bag for eloquence, courage, protection, and attaining desires.

Celestite—this is Sandra's number one stone for connecting to celestial forces. Add to a light-blue charm bag to communicate with angelic beings and spirit guides.

Chalcopyrite—this multicolored stone is sometimes called "peacock ore," but that name is meant to refer to a stone called bornite. Add to a white charm bag to clear blockages, open doors, and unlock hidden powers.

Chevron Amethyst—white quartz and amethyst combined, enhancing the qualities of both. Add to a purple charm bag to discover hidden abilities and talents, and level up by anticipating and eliminating issues in any situation.

Chrysocolla—a stone of hope, healing, and harmony, chrysocolla encourages level-headedness, clarity of thought, and patience. Add to a green charm bag to reduce anxiety and promote harmony and understanding.

Citrine—when we hear the phrase "pocket full of sunshine," we think of a handful of tumbled citrines. This is the stone we count on for creativity—we have worn it throughout the writing process of this very book. It helps to release negativity and build a confident outlook as well. Add to a gold charm bag for situations involving healing, business, money, psychic ability, or dreams.

Clear Quartz Crystal—this is the Swiss Army knife of the gemstone world. You can program a clear quartz crystal for any purpose, but it is especially powerful for psychic work, particularly for accessing the alpha brain wave state. Add to any charm bag to focus and energize your spells.

Coke Calcite—another workhorse for creatives, Coke calcite breaks through writer's block and lifts artists up out of a rut. It is also known to help people end unhealthy, unsatisfying relationships and leave dead-end jobs. Add to a black charm bag to cut ties and move on with confidence.

Dendritic Agate—a stone of the mind, bringing clarity, concentration, perception, and overall function, it is also associated with prosperity and status. Add to a gold charm bag to manifest opportunities to increase wealth and influence.

Desert Rose—formed from water, wind, and sand, desert rose can charge and cleanse other crystals. Native American lore states that these crystals were carved by warriors who returned from spirit to spread the roses across their homeland to protect it. Place in a black charm bag for powerful protection, and to keep the other crystals clear of residual negative energy.

Dragon's Blood Jasper—this mottled stone helps to build a thicker skin, and protects the physical as well as emotional bodies. Add to a red charm bag to attract sexual partners or a green charm bag for fertility.

Dumortierite—sometimes found within quartz, this third-eye opener is associated with lucid dreaming, astral travel, and channeling. Add to a purple charm bag to receive divine guidance and communicate psychically.

Emerald—there's an aura of abundance, prosperity, and luxury around these stones, which exude a lush, lavish energy. Add to a green charm bag to bring love, money, and more business.

Epidote—this stone turns up the volume on whatever it comes into contact with, so make sure you have defined your goals well when you use it. Add to any color charm bag to increase its power; add to a purple charm bag for lucid dreams.

Fancy Jasper—blast away feelings of guilt, gloom, fear, and doubt. Add to a white charm bag for emotional, mental, and physical healing.

Feather Agate—particularly useful to combat nightmares—tuck one into your pillowcase. Add to a red charm bag to protect your heart and boost your courage, whether you're asleep or awake.

Fossil Coral—wherever you roam, but especially if you will be traveling over water, take this stone with you for safety and blessings. Add to a black charm bag to protect and invite good luck in all life's storms.

Garnet—this bloodred gemstone is the mineral embodiment of passion and vitality. Add to a red charm bag for sex, healing, protection shields, vigor, and strength.

Garnet in Biotite (Black Mica)—this combination is next-level support for breaking bad habits and ending toxic relationships. Add to a red charm bag for physical strength, resilience, and vitality.

Grape Agate—this form of chalcedony is a must-have for anyone interested in dream magic. Add to a purple charm bag for prophetic dreams, visions, and intense meditation.

Green Kyanite—this supportive stone for heart-centered meditation can be used to tap into the spirit of nature; holding it and concentrating on reaching out to nature can feel as refreshing as walking through a lush forest. Add to a white charm bag to clear your space of negativity and bring yourself into alignment when you feel off-balance.

Green Onyx—useful in all matters concerning communication. Add to a silver charm bag to raise mental power and counteract the dreaded

Mercury retrograde, the period when the planet Mercury appears to be going backward, which is believed to cause interference and malfunctions relating to communication, travel, and technology.

Grossularite (Green Garnet)—all the power of red garnet, but with a more emotional, heart-driven energy. Add to a red charm bag for powerful regenerative healing, especially after heartbreak.

Hawk's Eye (Blue Tiger's Eye)—the old slogan "Don't leave home without it!" comes to mind: This stone is often carried by travelers for good luck. Add to a black charm bag to protect against psychic attacks.

Hematite—the weighted blanket of the mineral world, hematite provides deep, heavy grounding. Add to a black charm bag for energy balancing, or success in court.

Hematoid Quartz—this powerhouse combines the grounding force of hematite with the manifestation power of clear quartz crystal. Add to any charm bag to keep your feet firmly on the ground while manifesting your goals.

Howlite—one of the best stones if you are working on controlling eating habits, it can be added to a white charm bag to ease grief or a red charm bag for working on improving your health.

Hypersthene—when you make up your mind to turn over a new leaf, reach for this stone. Add to a white charm bag for purification of toxins and to promote transformation.

Icelandic Spar (Iceland Spar/Clear Calcite)—believed to be the stone the Vikings used to navigate on cloudy days, this stone has a reputation as a guide that persists to this day, and it brings insight and clarity to all situations. Add to a lavender charm bag for visions, prophetic dreams (especially those that provide guidance toward solutions to current issues), and communication with the higher realms.

Iolite—this rich violet gemstone plays well with others: It is often used in combination with other semiprecious stones in jewelry (such as citrine and peridot for financial and career success), but it is a dynamo all on its own. Add to a purple charm bag to attune to and communicate with spirit and/or the higher realms.

Jade—known the world over as a good-luck charm. Add jade to a green charm bag for love, healing, wisdom, longevity, and good fortune.

Jet—hundreds of millions of years old, this "stone" was created from the wood of trees transformed by water under intense pressure. One of the most famous varieties is Whitby jet, which is formed from the monkey puzzle tree in the United Kingdom. Add to a silver charm bag for skill in divination and to invoke the Great Goddess.

K2—named after the mountain it is mined from (which is the second highest point in the world), this crystal is a combination of azurite and granite. Add to a silver charm bag for meditation, lucid dreaming, and astral travel.

Kambaba Jasper—the swirling pattern of this stone is created by prehistoric algae—this is actually one of Earth's oldest fossils, believed to be responsible for the formation of our atmosphere. Add to a brown charm bag for animal communication and forming bonds with nature.

Labradorite—we consider labradorite, one of the most eye-catching stones due to its mesmerizing flash of nearly every color of the rainbow, to be an integral crystal for spirit communication. Wear around your neck or add to a silver charm bag to enhance divination, intuition, and mediumship.

Lapis Lazuli—opens the third eye and is associated with good fortune, intuition, and dreams (especially lucid dreaming), as well as communication with spirit guides and angels. Add to a royal blue charm bag for psychic ability, peacefulness, and spiritual love.

Larimar—called "the Atlantis stone" because it feels like the soul of the ocean. Add to a blue charm bag for relaxation, patience, emotional understanding, and healing from trauma.

Larvikite—sometimes mistakenly called "black labradorite" due to its shards of silvery-black feldspar, this essential stone for self-healing is particularly effective for people with anxiety and PTSD. Add to a red charm bag for protection and strength during stressful challenges.

Lava Rock—this solidified magma brings grounding, safety, and security, connects us to the earth, and gives us the power to bounce back from loss. Add to a brown charm bag for stress and anxiety relief.

Lemon Topaz—like the fruit it is named after, this gemstone energizes and stimulates; wear it when you need a pick-me-up. You can also add it to a gold charm bag for good luck and good fortune.

Lepidolite—we call this the "giggle stone" because holding it always makes us feel like laughing; it has lifted our spirits when we've been burdened with stress many times. Add to a lavender charm bag for peace, serenity, and protection from nightmares.

Lodolite—also called garden quartz due to the natural inclusions visible in it, this crystal can be added to a black charm bag to help release old patterns and break bad habits.

Malachite—this copper-based banded stone has so many benefits, it is a wise choice to be worn as jewelry or carried as part of your daily crystal practice. Add to a green charm bag for love, balance, or financial stability. It is also associated with protection, particularly of children.

Mookaite—have you ever felt "decision fatigue," where you have had to make so many judgment calls in a short period of time that you wish someone else would take over? Mookaite is your new BFF. Add to a red charm bag to help with that, as well as endurance, strength, vitality, and physical healing.

Moonstone—awaken the goddess within, and connect to the divine feminine with this gorgeous stone that comes in several luminous shades. The pearlescent white stones amplify Maiden energy: welcoming new beginnings, feeling beautiful, having enough energy to do all the things. Reddish/peach stones represent the gifts of the Mother: creative power, fertility in many forms, comfort in times of trial, and awesome strength. The darkest among these beauties are the Crone's jewels: time-tested wisdom, keen insight, and the peace that comes with acceptance of brutal truths. As part of your daytime routine, rock the foresight to make better choices. At night, expect prophecy in your dreams. Add to a silver charm bag for divination, Moon magic, psychic ability, and diet.

Moss Agate—this form of chalcedony was obviously named based on the mossy inclusions it contains; each one looks like a miniature fairy forest. It helps grow the good things in life, like health, wealth, confidence, and success, as well as your garden. Add to a green charm bag to strengthen your green thumb, or for swift recovery from illness or injury.

Nuummite—the deep, mysterious iridescent flecks in this darkest-brown-to-black metamorphic rock look a bit like outer space. Add to any charm bag to supply it with continuous energy and protect your magic.

Obsidian—this stone is the classic choice for crystal scrying mirrors. One of the most effective protections against negativity, it can be added to a black charm bag to deflect or reflect any psychic attack.

Ocean Jasper—when you visit the beach, the negative ions in the air refresh you. Ocean jasper is the crystal equivalent of this feeling. Add to a pink charm bag as a mood booster, to help navigate emotional issues, and heal past traumas.

Opalite—it is a man-made stone, but we have used it as an effective meditation tool as well as a spell focus. Add to a pink charm bag to work on self-love, improve mood, and attract business.

Orange Calcite—it's like a vitamin C booster for your sex life! Add to a red charm bag for confidence and sexual prowess, or a green charm bag for fertility.

Peridot—born of fire and brought to light; formed not in the crust of the earth but in the molten rock of the upper mantle, the domain of earthquakes and volcanos, some peridot may even be extraterrestrial. It has the power of regeneration, and helps us discover our purpose in this life and break blockages and addictions. Add to a green charm bag for abundance, health, wealth, joy, and love.

Petrified Wood—this plant-based fossil links you with your soul's history, as well as the soul of nature. Add to a brown charm bag for past-life recall and to connect to flora and fauna spirits.

Picasso Jasper—this stone is especially useful for creatives; it helps strike a balance between letting the imagination run wild and keeping one's feet on the ground. Add to a gold charm bag to support a positive mind-set and increase creativity.

Pink Jasper—the warm, gentle vibe of this stone is one of contentment. Add to a pink charm bag to heal relationship traumas and find hope after heartache.

Pink Opal—this stone facilitates cooperation, compassion, generosity . . . all of the traits that would restore your faith in humanity! Add to a pink charm bag for emotional healing and balance, comfort, and inner peace.

Pink Tourmaline—effective for anxiety relief and emotional healing, especially in cases of PTSD. Add to a pink charm bag to soothe emotional pain, quiet anxiety, and ease worry.

Poppy Jasper—associated with controlling and stimulating energy, mental activity, and sex drive. Add to a red charm bag for lust, physical endurance, motivation, and power.

Prehnite with Epidote—this dream combo pairs prehnite, which enhances precognition and mental preparedness, with epidote, which soothes, strengthens, and supports. Add to a white charm bag for powerful healing and balance of body, mind, and soul.

Pyrite—this is the substance that was nicknamed "fool's gold," but it has been used to increase genuine wealth. Add to a gold charm bag for prosperity, divination, and good luck.

Rainbow Fluorite—this is our MVP for writing because it keeps us focused and facilitates the flow of ideas. Add to an indigo charm bag to enhance mental awareness and perceptive ability.

Rainbow Moonstone—when labradorite is in a white matrix (rather than charcoal gray), it's known as rainbow moonstone, and it has the same intense color play as well as the affinity with the spirit world.

Add to a lavender charm bag for psychic protection, calm sleep, and to ease trauma.

Rainbow Obsidian—the full spectrum of light is reflected in the color bands of this stone, and all of the psychic information carried by that light is absorbed when this stone is worn or carried. Add to a black charm bag to help get into an alpha brain wave state for psychic power.

Red Calcite—when you feel your motivation draining away, red calcite will get you back on track. Add to a red charm bag to increase your energy levels to achieve your goals.

Red Jasper—when Sandra had major surgery, this was one of three stones she carried into the hospital for its healing and fortifying properties. Add to a red charm bag for defensive magic, and to send harmful energy back to the sender.

Red Malachite—the concentration of iron in this stone turns it red; the strength of that iron is reflected in the stone's ability to support anyone who wears or carries it in their daily battles. Add to a red charm bag for courage and determination, especially to fight addiction.

Red Tiger's Eye—a stone of confidence, motivation, strength, courage, and vitality. Add to a red charm bag to enhance those traits or a black charm bag to protect against all attacks and reveal hidden enemies.

Rhodochrosite—there's an innocence, a purity of spirit, to this crystal. It encourages us to have hope, to see things with the eyes of a child. Add to a pink charm bag to heal the wounds of the past, including those of your ancestors.

Rhodonite—the stark contrast between the pink and black in this stone reflects its ability to balance the light and darkness within ourselves, and reminds us to practice self-compassion. It soothes us in times of stress and supports our efforts to forgive and forget. Add to a red charm bag to be calm in chaos, and cast off confusion and doubt.

Rose Quartz—love, sweet love . . . if you're looking for the kind that messes up your lipstick but not your mascara, you want at least one rose quartz in your arsenal. And if you do end up in a fight, this crystal is the one that you should reach for to melt tension, foster understanding, and facilitate forgiveness. Rose quartz is a powerhouse stone for self-care; you gotta love yourself first before you can truly love somebody else. Add to a pink charm bag for love, self-esteem, joy, marriage, and friendship.

Rutilated Quartz—one of Sandra's favorites! Add to any charm bag to bring powerful manifestation and success energy.

Scolecite—meditate with this stone to completely wipe the day's slate clean. Add to a red charm bag to recharge your energy and power through challenges.

Selenite—this is the crystal equivalent to a power washer! Add to any charm bag to purify a space and keep other crystals free of negativity.

Serpentine—corrects mental and emotional imbalances. Add to a red charm bag to protect from poison and to protect nursing mothers, or a black charm bag to feel more in control. Add to a purple charm bag to access past-life memories to aid in overcoming current challenges.

Shungite—used to purify water as well as energy, this stone contains fullerenes, which are detoxifying via carbon and antioxidants. Add to a black charm bag for powerful protection from outer forces, including electromagnetic fields.

Smoky Quartz—when you can't burn sage to clear a space, reach for smoky quartz. Basically a vacuum cleaner that sucks up negativity, it is a strong ally in the war on drama. It connects you to your ancestors, and they don't suffer fools. If you fly off the handle, smoky quartz will bring you back to center and ground your thoughts in reality. If you have a tendency to overthink, try wearing this where you can see it or carry it where you can hold it when you sense yourself analyzing something to death. Add to a black charm bag for mood elevation, grounding, protection, and positivity.

Snowflake Obsidian—the stark combination of black and white reveals the truth, and helps us with shadow work (acknowledging the darker aspects of ourselves, and healing those who need it). Formed from cooling lava, this stone can be added to a red charm bag to call on the energy of the volcano to protect you.

Sodalite—the mineral MVP when it comes to harmony, peacekeeping, and cooperation. It helps to verbalize feelings. Add to a white charm bag to keep the peace, or a blue charm bag to aid in healing stress, anger, and fear.

Stromatolite—slow and steady wins the race; this fossil teaches us patience and is a problem solver's best buddy. Add to a purple charm bag to access past-life memories and ancestral wisdom to assist with current hurdles.

Sunstone—SPF for the soul and vitamin C for the spirit, this stone can help us make peace with the past by letting go of painful memories. It brings the energy of the whimsy of childhood into the present Add to a gold charm bag for protection, health (especially mental health), and to honor the solar gods.

Tiger's Eye—when you're anxious, you need more than something to settle your nerves. While other stones boast calming effects, tiger's eye is all about courage, strength, and stability. It brings a sense of balance when everything around you feels chaotic. In ancient times, it was carried as a talisman of protection from curses and jealousy. Basically, haters gonna hate, but they can't dull your shine or ruin your good mood when you have this stone on your side. Add to a gold charm bag for money, courage, luck, and protection against the evil eye.

Tree Agate—add to a green charm bag to restore energy, relax, and connect deeply with nature.

Turquoise—this powerful stone blends all the classical elements: the color of water, the energy of both fire and air, and the strength of Earth. It protects travelers. Add to a green charm bag for good luck, healing, and spiritual growth.

Unakite—the trio of pink feldspar, epidote, and quartz come together to form this unique crystal. Add to a pink charm bag to help release anger, bitterness, and regret.

Zebra Jasper—this stone is typically more blotchy than striped, but it got its name from the stark contrast of its black and white composition. Add one to a blue charm bag to enhance wisdom, see the truth, and remain hopeful.

Sources

Armády, Naha, *Everyday Crystal Rituals: Healing Practices for Love, Wealth, Career, and Home*, Emeryville, CA: Althea Press, 2018.

"Aventurine Meaning & Healing Properties," Energy Muse, accessed March 10, 2021, https://www.energymuse.com/aventurine-meaning.

Cunningham, Scott, *Cunningham's Encyclopedia of Crystal, Gem & Metal Magic*, 2nd ed., St. Paul, MN: Llewellyn Publications, 2003.

Frazier, Karen, *Crystals for Healing: The Complete Reference Guide with Over 200 Remedies for Mind, Heart & Soul*, Berkeley, CA: Althea Press, 2015.

Harding, Jennie, *Crystals*, New York, NY: Chartwell Books, 2016.

"Learn About Crystals," The Crystal Council, 2018, https://thecrystalcouncil.com/crystals.

Melody, *Love Is in the Earth: A Kaleidoscope of Crystals: The Reference Book Describing the Metaphysical Properties of the Mineral Kingdom*, Wheatridge, CO: Earth-Love Publishing, 1995.

"Peridot Meaning and Uses," Crystal Vaults, accessed March 4, 2021, https://www.crystalvaults.com/crystal-encyclopedia/peridot.

Simmons, Robert, and Naisha Ahsian, *The Book of Stones: Who They Are and What They Teach*, 3rd ed., Berkeley, CA: North Atlantic Books, 2015.

Thornton, John, "May Gem Stones—Emerald, Chrysocolla, Moss Agate, Sapphire, Carnelian, Aquamarine, Sardonyx, Chalcedony," Great Conjunction Spiritual Center, accessed March 2, 2021, https://greatconjunction.org/gemstones/may-gem-stones.

Also by

SANDRA MARIAH WRIGHT
and **LEANNE MARRAMA**

An Intuitive Guide to the Ancient Art
and Modern Magic of Tea Leaf Divination

Sandra Mariah Wright & Leanne Marrama

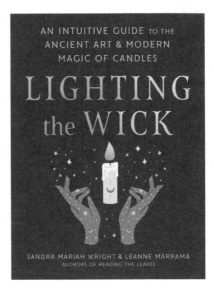

AN INTUITIVE GUIDE TO THE
ANCIENT ART & MODERN
MAGIC OF CANDLES

LIGHTING
the WICK

SANDRA MARIAH WRIGHT & LEANNE MARRAMA
AUTHORS OF *READING THE LEAVES*

tarcherperigee